Plastics — Craft and Design

A. Yarwood

Nelson

Thomas Nelson and Sons Ltd.
36 Park Street London W1Y 4DE
P.O. Box 18123 Nairobi Kenya
Thomas Nelson (Australia) Ltd.
19–39 Jeffcott Street West Melbourne Victoria 3003
Thomas Nelson and Sons (Canada) Ltd.
81 Curlew Drive Don Mills Ontario
Thomas Nelson (Nigeria) Ltd.
P.O. Box 336 Apapa Lagos

© A. Yarwood 1975
First published 1975
ISBN 0 17 431050 1

Filmset by Filmtype Services Limited, Scarborough, Yorkshire
Printed by A. Wheaton & Co. Ltd., Exeter

Contents

Acknowledgements

The author wishes to place on record his grateful appreciation of the assistance given to him by the members of the following firms who supplied information from which he was able to ascertain the accuracy of details contained in this book.

Any errors of fact which have occurred are the fault of the author in interpreting the information so freely and generously given.

Bakelite Xylonite Limited
B.P. Chemicals International Limited
G. H. Bloore Limited
Bondaglass Voss Limited
Cornelius Chemical Company Limited
Crafts Unlimited
Dunlop Limited
Imperial Chemical Industries Limited
Rohm and Haas (U.K.) Limited
Shell Chemicals (U.K.) Limited
Alec Tiranti Limited
Trylon Limited

In particular Trylon Limited not only supplied information but also allowed the author to photograph articles made from polyesters and fibre glass in their showrooms at Wollaston.

This book is dedicated to the author's daughter, Jean, without whose help the work involved would not have been possible.

Preface

Those new materials grouped under the term 'plastics' are rapidly becoming important for craft and art teaching in schools. Teachers have become interested in the possibilities of these new materials and are experimenting with methods of using them to express ideas in craft and art forms. The increasing popularity of plastics in craft education reflects the growing importance of plastics generally. Because plastics lend themselves to so many applications, the curiosity and interest of pupils in these materials is aroused even before they commence work in them. Teachers are wisely taking advantage of this interest.

One of the most important reasons for teaching any craft is that, apart from the craft techniques learned, an appreciation of the artistic value of well designed craft work is inevitably absorbed by pupils as they practice the craft. Such appreciation should lead to attempts by pupils to develop new designs in the materials in which they work. It is the author's contention that plastic materials provide an ideal medium for fostering the appreciation of the artistic and design possibilities of craft work generally. By their very nature plastics enable new forms to be produced rapidly and easily. Plastics are also in good supply and relatively cheap. There can be a direct design link between formal art and craft as taught in the schools via craft work in plastics. This design link seems to be somewhat easier to establish when relating craft work in plastics to art studies, than when attempting the link between pure art and such crafts as woodwork or metalwork. This is because the details of line, form, shape and colour often considered in art studies can so quickly be applied to work in plastics when used in craft studies. The true relationship between craft and art can be speedily recognized by pupils working in these materials. This recognition must surely assist in strengthening the art/craft bonds in other crafts.

The aim of this book is to show how varied and interesting work in plastic materials can be made by pupils in secondary school design courses. No attempt has been made to lay down a course which should be rigidly followed. Rather, it is hoped that the variety of methods shown here will spark off interest in adapting these methods to different work of reasonably original design. Quite apart from the methods of working in plastics which are described, the general underlying theory of plastic materials — where they originate, how they are made, how they are used industrially — have also been described. As much detail has been included in the theoretical pages as is considered necessary when teaching craft work in plastics.

1 Introduction to Plastics

Clay and 'Plasticine' are plastic. This means they may be pressed or moulded into shapes which are then retained. These two materials are not, however, 'plastics' in the modern sense of the term. Today a material is called a 'plastic' if it is one of the wide range of man-made materials all of which are products of the chemical industry. 'Plastics' are the results of reactions between chemical compounds which have been derived from such raw materials as wood, coal, cotton, crude oil, natural gas, air, water, salt and limestone. These products are indeed plastic at some stage in their manufacture, hence the use of the term. A few examples are given:

Derivation of some plastics from raw materials

Monomers   Polymers

Polythene (polyethylene) – a thermoplastic

Crude oil

Natural gas

    ————————————————ethylene————polyethylene

Air

Water

PVC (polyvinyl chloride) – a thermoplastic

Crude oil

Natural gas

    ——————————ethylene————vinyl chloride———polyvinyl

Air   chloride

Water

Common salt ——————————chlorine

Melamine (melamine formaldehyde) – a thermosetting plastic

Coal

Air ——carbon monoxide———methanol——formaldehyde

Water   melamine formaldehyde

Limestone ——calcium cyanamide——dicyanodiamide——melamine

As can be seen from the three examples quoted above, plastics are derived from organic compounds. Organic compounds always contain some carbon. The molecules of organic compounds each contain no more than 100 atoms. Each molecule of a plastic contains many thousands of atoms. Crude oil, natural gas, air, water, salt, limestone etc. whose molecules contain a relatively small number of atoms are called *monomers*. The plastic materials which contain molecules with atoms numbered in thousands are called *polymers*. The chemical reaction of changing monomers into polymers is called *polimerization*. The atoms of polymer molecules are arranged in long chains or in large three-dimensional masses.

Two main groups of plastics

Thermoplastics

If the atoms of individual molecules of a plastic are arranged in long chains thus:

the material is a *thermoplastic*. If a thermoplastic is heated it will become plastic and malleable. While hot it can be moulded into a required shape. Upon cooling to room temperature the shape is retained and the plastic becomes firm. If the cooled plastic is then reheated it can be remoulded into a totally different shape.

Thermosetting plastics

If the atoms of individual molecules of a plastic are arranged with the long chains interlinked with each other in all three dimensions thus:

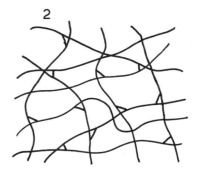

the material is a *thermo-setting* plastic. Thermo-setting plastics, once shaped, cannot be remoulded after heating. Once set, or fully polymerized, the material will never assume a plastic or malleable state again.

Some thermoplastics and common applications

Polythene (polyethylene) — Low density (LDPE) — transparent packing materials in bag or sheet form; washing-up bottles. High density (HDPE) — washing-up bowls; moulds for polyester castings; bleach bottles.

Polypropylene (PP) — Hinges for plastic boxes; ship's ropes; fishing nets.

Polyvinyl chloride (PVC) — Rigid — guttering and rain pipes; gramophone records; roofing sheets. Plasticised — cable sheathing; hose pipes; upholstery.

Polystyrene (PS) — Food containers; disposable cups; storage boxes.

Expanded polystyrene (EPS) — Ceiling tiles; packaging of fragile articles such as cameras.

Acrylonitrile butadiene styrene (ABS) — Casings for food mixers; radio and television knobs.

Cellulose acetate (CA) — Photographic film.

Cellulose acetate butyrate (CAB) — Chisel and screwdriver handles.

Cellulose nitrate (CN) — Table tennis balls.

Polyester film (P) — Recording tapes. This thermoplastic which is manufactured from polyethylene terephthalate should not be confused with the thermosetting polyester resins.

Acrylics (PMMA) — 'Perspex' — Illumination signs; street lamps; scooter windshields.

Nylon (N) — Curtain rail fittings; hinges; casings for power tools such as drills.

Polytetrafluoro-ethylene (PTFE) — Non-stick coatings for cooking utensils; plumber's pipe sealing tape.

Acetal (A) — 'Kangol' seat belt buckles.

Polyurethane foam (PU) — Upholstery padding for furniture; mattresses in caravans.

Some thermosetting plastics and common applications

Urea formaldehyde (UF) — Electric fittings of a light colour.

Phenol formaldehyde (PF) — Electric fittings of a dark colour. Domestic hot iron handles; saucepan handles.

Melamine formaldehyde (MF) — 'Melaware' crockery; top layer of 'Formica' laminate.

Polyester resin (PR) — The resin of fibre glass (GRP — glass reinforced plastic).

Epoxy resin — Supplied as a two-resin packet to be mixed together for gluing.

Simple identification tests

These tests can be used to identify the plastics listed above, all of which are in fairly common use at the present time. Plastics other than those named may be found. There are five simple tests as follows. The results of the tests are given below.

1　Feel the surface, try to bend the sample, try to scratch the surface with a finger nail.

2　Drop a small sample into water which contains a few drops of washing-up liquid.

3　Cut the sample with a knife or with scissors.

4　Try to burn a small sample held in tongs or tweezers over a small flame. Take *great care* not to let any molten plastic fall on to clothes or hands.

5　Gently sniff the odour caused by burning. Be *very cautious* — some plastics give off irritating fumes.

Results of tests

1	Flexible, soft	LDPE; PVC(p); PU
	Stiff, hard	HDPE; PP; PVC(r); PS (metallic ring when tapped); ABS; PMMA; N
	Hard but flexible	CA; CAB; CN; P; A
	Smooth, slippery, fairly soft	PTFE
	Stiff, hard, solid	UF; PF; MF; PR

2	Sample floats	LDPE; HDPE; PP; EPS; PU
	Sample sinks	PVC(r or p); PS; ABS; CA; CAB; CN; P; PMMA; N; PTFE; A; UF; PF; MF; PR
3	Cuts easily leaving smooth edges	LDPE; HDPE; PP; PVC(r and p); ABS; CA; CN; PF; N; PTFE; A; PU (does not crumble)
	Difficult to cut	PS; EPS (crumbles); PMMA (splinters); UF (flakes); PF (flakes); MF (flakes); PR (brittle)
4	Flame and colour even after source of heat removed:	
	Blue flame with yellow tip	LDPE; HDPE; N (difficult to ignite)
	Yellow flame	PVC(p); CN; P; PMMA; PU
	Orange yellow flame	PS; EPS; ABS
	Dark yellow flame	CA; CAB
	Yellow flame with trace of blue at bottom	PP
	Very pale, almost invisible blue	A
	Flame goes out when source of heat removed; difficult to burn	PVC(r); UF; PF; MF
	Little smoke with flame	LDPE; HDPE; PMMA; N; A
	Some smoke	CA; CAB; CN
	Smoky flame	PS (black sooty smuts); EPS (black sooty smuts); ABS; P; PR
	Sample swells, cracks and turns white at edges of burnt portion	UF; MF
5	Odour:	
	Burning candle	LDPE; HDPE; PP
	Acrid – hydrochloric acid	PVC
	Marigold-like smell	PVC
	Bitter but rubbery	ABS
	Rancid	CAB
	Vinegary	CA
	Camphor (mothballs)	CN
	Like raspberry jam	P
	Fruity	PMMA; PR
	Burning hair	N
	Pungent, formaldehyde	A; UF (fishy); MF (fishy)
	Acrid	PU
	Carbolic	PF

Some additional features not already given

When alight, molten droplets which extinguish on reaching floor	LDPE; HDPE
Melts to a free flowing liquid carrying its flame with it	N
Will not ignite in ordinary flame	PTFE

Note: Bottles and packets must be thoroughly cleaned if used for testing, as burning and odour results may be affected by the contents clinging to the plastic samples.

Storage of plastic materials

Some plastics once ignited will continue to burn for some time; a few will degrade or discolour if exposed for long periods to direct sunlight. Sheet thermoplastic materials may distort out of shape if stored in a warm and unventilated atmosphere. Because of such factors, if a fair amount of work in plastic materials is envisaged, the material should be stored in a cool, well ventilated, dry, brick-built store which does not allow the access of direct sunlight. Such a store is of particular importance in respect of the storage of polyester resins and their associated chemicals. Polyester resins, while not being highly inflammable, do present some degree of fire risk. If kept in warm, sunny conditions their storage life (shelf life) may be considerably reduced. They should therefore be stored in cool conditions and kept in light-proof containers such as tins, steel drums or dark plastic containers. Catalysts (hardeners) and cleaning fluids should be stored apart from the resins. Catalysts should be in air vented bottles about half full to allow gases to escape. If activators (accelerators) are also stored, these should be in a different place to the catalysts and resins. Pre-activated resins should normally not be stored for more than a few months because they may set hard if kept for more than some six months. If they are still liquid, however, they remain usable.

Safety precautions

1   When testing to identify plastics, molten drops must not be allowed to fall on clothes or skin.

2   When testing odours to identify plastics remember that some plastic fumes are noxious.

3   Good ventilation of the working area is essential.

4   When machining, sawing or sanding it is advisable to wear a face mask and goggles. Dust and fumes can be irritating to throat and eyes.

5   When cutting expanded polystyrene with a hot wire cutter styrene fumes are given off. These fumes can irritate the eyes and even cause drowsiness. Therefore allow adequate ventilation. Do not allow the wire to run red hot.

6   When working with polyester resins and glass fibre the following precautions should be taken.

(a) Always use a barrier cream on the hands. Any risk of dermatitis is then eliminated.

(b) If glass fibre irritates the hands apply barrier cream and wear disposable polythene gloves or rubber gloves.

(c) *Never, under any circumstances*, mix together catalyst and activator. The mixture may be explosive.

(d) If catalyst gets into the eyes wash the eyes thoroughly with plenty of water. *Then consult a doctor.* Catalyst can irritate and burn the skin. Wash off immediately with plenty of water.

(e) Waste catalysed resin can generate enough heat to start a fire. Place such waste in metal containers or dowse in cold water. Do not place among rags or papers.

(f) The cleaners used for cleaning off uncured resin are very inflammable. Be careful with the disposal of rags impregnated with such cleaning fluid. Do not use these cleaners to clean the hands. They act as degreasers. Wash the hands in soap and water or use special hand cleaning creams.

7 If making up polyurethane foam from chemicals work in the open air. The toxic gases will then be carried away from the area.

8 No smoking can be allowed when working with polyester resins.

Plastics for craft work

The plastics listed below can be obtained in small quantities for craft working. A list of suppliers is shown on pages 93 to 96. Typical examples of craft use are shown against each plastic named, together with some simple details of the properties of the plastics.

Polythene − sheets for protection when working in polyester resins or for making moulds for illuminated panels. Powders for dip coating of metals. Thermoplastic. Light in weight, tough and flexible. Excellent electrical insulator. Good resistance to chemicals. No release agent required when used with polyester resins.

Polypropylene − thin sheets for vacuum forming. A rigid thermoplastic. Range of colours. Tough and odourless. Resists boiling water. Excellent chemical resistance − thus cannot be easily painted. Jointing by hot welding with polypropylene rod. Its unique flexing qualities make it valuable for hinging box lids. Excellent electrical insulator. Cementing not practicable.

PVC (polyvinyl chloride) − thin sheets for vacuum forming. Coatings to fabrics (plasticized). Flexible tubes (plasticized). Thermoplastic. Rigid pvc is rigid up to about 60°C. Easily stretched and bent from about 90°C to about 120°C. Decomposes above about 130°C. Self extinguishing − when flame is removed, burning stops. Jointing by hot air welding or with special pvc cements. Sharp corners or turns are a source of weakness, possibly causing splits in rigid pvc sheet.

Expanded polystyrene − sheets and blocks for three-dimensional letters, contour models for geography, model aeroplane parts, large jigsaw puzzles, sculpture profiles. Thermoplastic. Soft and very light in weight. White in colour. Crumbles when cut by knife but can be cleanly cut with a hot wire operating between about 200°C and 400°C. Very cheap and easily available from packings. Dissolves if cellulose paint is applied or under the action of polyester resins. Can be painted with emulsion paints which then give protection against polyester resins.

Polyester film − 'Melinex'. Gives smooth surface to polyesters when applied at gel stage. Thermoplastic. Tough and flexible transparent film with great mechanical strength. Excellent electrical insulator. High chemical resistance.

Acrylics (polymethyl methacrylate) − 'Perspex', 'Oroglas', 'Plexiglas' etc. Light shades, simple jewellery such as rings, bangles, pendants, serviette rings, salad servers. Thermoplastic. Sheets and bars of various sections. Transparent water clear, tinted and opaque. Excellent weathering qualities. Excellent optical qualities. Good electrical insulator. Rigid up to 85°C, malleable and easily bent and stretched from about 100°C to about 150°C. Machined or hand worked as for aluminium but with zero or negative top rake on machine tools. Cemented with 'Tensol' No. 6 or 7 or other acrylic cements. Tough and not easily broken but may split at sharp corners. Slow burning, but smoulders after flame is removed.

Nylon (polyamide) − sheets, rods and blocks for machining. Usually cream or white in colour. Light in weight. A rigid thermoplastic. Excellent frictional and wear properties. Absorbs or loses water in response to changes in atmospheric humidity. Cementing impracticable. Jointing must be mechanical. Machines well with negative or zero top rake on tools and copious coolant (water or water soluble oils). Melting point about 260°C (Nylon 66). Fairly good electrical insulator at low voltages. Excellent resistance to oils and fuels. Can be worked with hand metalwork tools.

Polyester resins − very wide range of craft uses, particularly with glass fibre to form shapes in GRP (glass reinforced plastic). Wide range of liquid-like resins available from thin to thick (thixotropic) and of differing transparencies and setting times for different applications. Resins set solid (polymerize) at room temperatures. Thermosetting. Hard and brittle, but when reinforced with fibre glass or other materials becomes tough and will withstand hard blows and flexing without damage. A very versatile craft plastic.

Epoxy resins – useful in craft work because the resin will cement together practically any known material. This is because these resins set at room temperature and do not shrink as they set. They will adhere to most substances in common use. Used also as filled resins in car body repair work. Thermosetting.

Polyurethane foam – blocks of foam for upholstery. Rigid polyurethane for base structure of polyester sculpture or to give buoyancy to canoes. Upholstery foams easily available in a variety of hardnesses (densities). Thermoplastic. Soft and flexible, easily cut by sharp knife. Highly inflammable with very toxic fumes unless specially treated. Rigid foam can be easily shaped with woodwork or metalwork tools or with knives. Very light in weight.

Urea formaldehyde – wood glues such as 'Cascamite One Shot'. Thermosetting.

Phenol formaldehyde – backing sheets of plastic laminate sheet material such as 'Formica'. Thermosetting. Brown in colour. Hard and tough. Can be cut by scoring or with hacksaws and shaped with metalwork files.

2 Methods of Production

The drawings on this page and on pages 12 and 13 are diagrammatic. They are only intended to illustrate the principles involved in the processes being described.

Vacuum forming

A method of shaping thin thermoplastic sheets. The thermoplastic sheet is firmly clamped flat between two sides of some form of holder and then warmed by heaters until it is in a rubber-like, malleable state. The heaters are swung to one side and the warmed, malleable sheet brought into contact with a mould by forming a vacuum between the sheet and the mould. The vacuum is produced by suction from a vacuum pump, either a mechanical or a hand pump. The resulting pressure forces the sheet to drape exactly over or into the mould. Air cooling takes place quite rapidly, and when the article is cool it can be taken off the mould. Either male or female moulds may be used, depending mainly on which is the easier to make. Machines of this type are quite suitable for craft work. Illustrations of a craft-made vacuum forming machine are shown on pages 14 to 16.

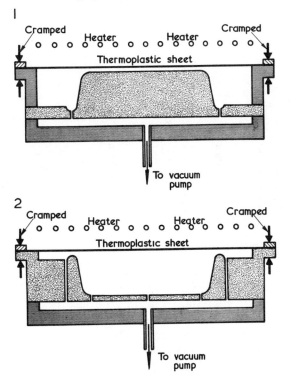

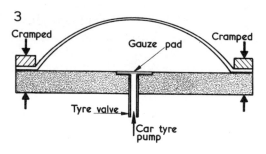

3

Cramped

Gauze pad

Cramped

Tyre valve

Car tyre pump

Free blow moulding

A method of forming thermoplastic sheets into domed shapes. The method is usually restricted to acrylics. The thermoplastic sheet is heated in an oven and then rapidly cramped into holders in the machine. Compressed air is then blown under the sheet. This forces the sheet into a domed shape which is retained on cooling. The apparatus itself needs to be warmed to about 50°C to prevent chilling of the plastic sheet as it is cramped in place. Free blow moulding machines can be craft made. Compressed air can be obtained from a car tyre pump connected to a tyre valve in the machine.

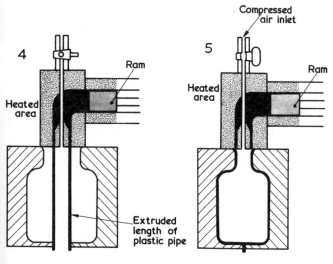

4

Heated area

Ram

5

Compressed air inlet

Heated area

Ram

Extruded length of plastic pipe

Blow moulding

An industrial method for producing bottles and other hollow containers from thermoplastic materials. Plastic granules or chips are fed to a heated area in the machine into which a ram is forced. The resulting pressure and heat changes the granules into a malleable, dough-like mass. Suitable dies

fixed to the outlet of the machine allow lengths of hollow pipe to be extruded into the space between two sides of a split mould. While the plastic is still hot, the split mould is closed and compressed air passed into the mould. This forces the malleable plastic against the mould walls to produce the required container. When cool, the mould is opened and the container released.

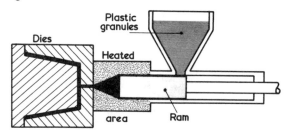

6

Plastic granules

Dies

Heated

area

Ram

Injection moulding

This is the most widely used industrial method of producing articles from thermoplastics. Plastic granules are fed from a hopper into a cylinder in which a ram works. The ram forces the granules through a heated area where, under the action of the heat and pressure, the plastic melts. Each stroke of the ram forces a known quantity of the molten plastic into a mould. Pressure is maintained for a short period, and the ram is then withdrawn and the mould opened. This cycle is repeated to produce a continuous succession of identical mouldings.

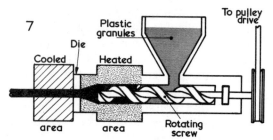

7

Plastic granules

To pulley drive

Die

Cooled

Heated

area

area

Rotating screw

Extrusion

An industrial method of producing pipes, rods of various profiles, sheets and filaments from thermoplastics. A continuously revolving screw within a cylinder drives thermoplastic granules through a heated area. The pressure and heat cause the plastic to melt. The molten plastic is extruded through suitable dies which determine the profile of the section of the extruded material. The extrusion is passed through a cooling area before being fed away from the machine on rollers or fed on to drums.

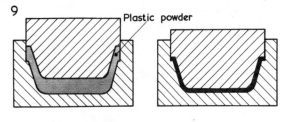

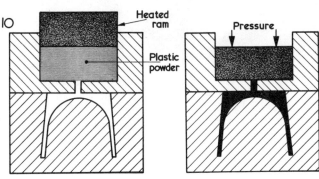

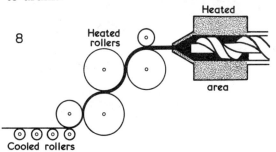

Calendering

This is an extrusion method of producing thin sheet material from thermoplastics. Polythene and pvc sheet is produced by calendering. A ribbon of heated plastic is fed from an extruder over heated and polished rollers. The sheet is successively made thinner by being passed between suitably spaced rollers before being fed away on cooled rollers.

Transfer and compression moulding

These two industrial processes are used mainly for the production of mouldings made from the thermosetting plastics urea formaldehyde, phenol formaldehyde and melamine formaldehyde. In *transfer moulding* uncured thermosetting powders are heated and then forced under pressure into suitable moulds. The heat and pressure cause polymerization to take place. In *compression moulding* the thermosetting powder is placed between suitably shaped parts of a split mould which is closed under heat and pressure. Polymerization is completed under the action of the heat and pressure, so cooling is not required. The moulded article can be released from the machine while still hot.

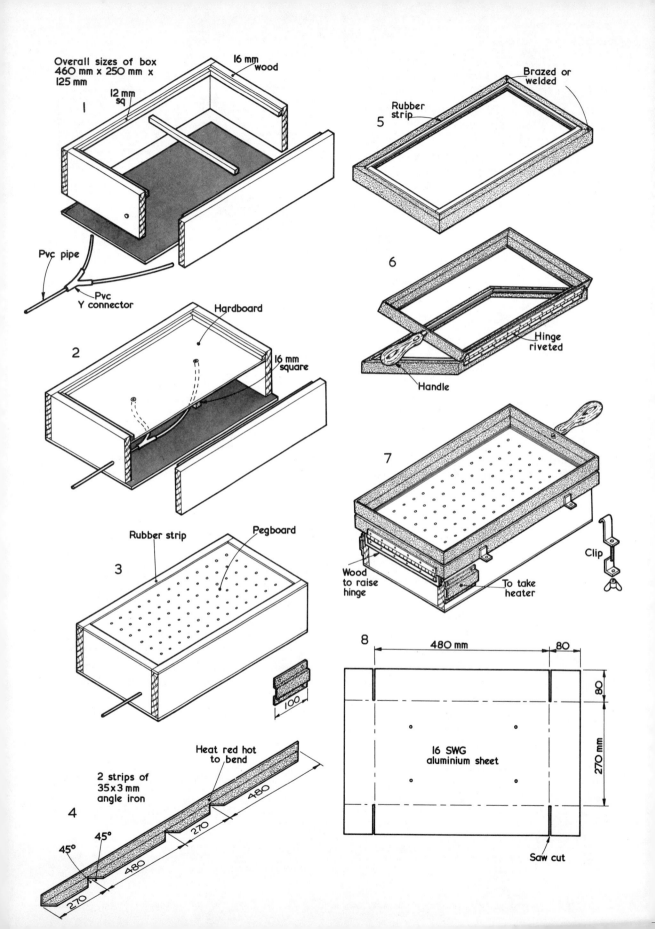

1 Overall sizes of box 460 mm x 250 mm x 125 mm

16 mm wood

12 mm sq

Pvc pipe

Pvc Y connector

2 Hardboard

16 mm square

3 Rubber strip

Pegboard

100

4 2 strips of 35 x 3 mm angle iron

Heat red hot to bend

480

45°

45°

45°

270

480

270

480

5 Rubber strip

Brazed or welded

6 Hinge riveted

Handle

7 Wood to raise hinge

To take heater

Clip

8 480 mm

80

80

270 mm

16 SWG aluminium sheet

Saw cut

3 Some Plastics Machines

Vacuum forming machine

This machine can be made with comparative ease and may be used to vacuum form thermoplastic sheet up to about 1·5 mm thick – pvc, polypropylene and acrylic. The drawings 1 to 9 show the method of making the machine. The vacuum forming source may be either a powered vacuum pump or a hand pump.

Drawing 1. A box is made from 16 mm thick wood. Corners of the box can be glued and nailed. Strips of wood each 12 mm square are glued and pinned inside, 3 mm below the top edges of the box. Lengths of flexible pvc piping with a 5 mm bore are joined to a pvc Y-shaped connector.

Drawing 2. Before fixing the bottom, glue and pin 3 mm thick hardboard under the 12 mm square strips. A strengthening strip 16 mm square may be glued to the underside of the hardboard to stiffen it against the action of the vacuum formed above it.

Drawing 3. Glue and pin pegboard to the upper edges of the 12mm square strips.
Glue strips of rubber from an inner tube with Evostick around the top edges of the box. Make two brackets from steel sheet and screw to each side of the box.

Drawing 4. Two strips of angle iron are sawn and shaped, using hacksaw and files. These are heated and bent to form two rectangular frames as in Drawing 5.

Drawing 5. The corners of the angle iron rectangles are brazed or welded to make strong frames. Strips of rubber are glued to the flat side of each frame.

Drawing 6. The two steel frames are hinged to each other by rivetting a length of steel piano hinge in place. A handle is screwed to the top frame with a stout wood screw from inside the frame. The thermoplastic sheet is held between the two parts of this hinged cramping device.

Drawing 7. The complete machine except for the heater. The sheet cramp is hinged to the box via a strip of wood, and clips are made to hold the two parts of the cramp together. The lower part of each clip is brazed or rivetted to the lower frame. Wing nuts provide a means of quickly cramping and releasing the plastic sheet.

Drawing 8. A piece of aluminium sheet is cut to shape as shown, then bent and rivetted to form a heater box as shown in Drawing 9.

Drawing 9. Two L-shaped brackets are rivetted to the sides of the aluminium box. A piece of asbestos sheet is shaped and slotted to enable a 2 kW electric wire heater to be wound in and out to form a heater element. This element is bolted via metal tubes to the aluminium box, and leads from the element are connected to an electric plug. The body of the box should be connected to the earth point of the plug.

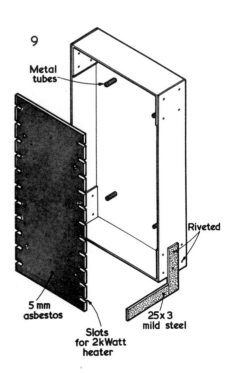

9

Metal tubes

5 mm asbestos

Slots for 2kWatt heater

Riveted

25 x 3 mild steel

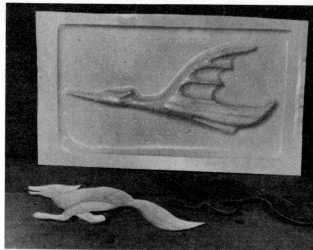

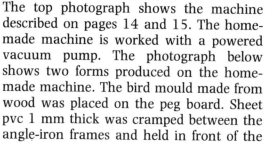

The top photograph shows the machine described on pages 14 and 15. The home-made machine is worked with a powered vacuum pump. The photograph below shows two forms produced on the home-made machine. The bird mould made from wood was placed on the peg board. Sheet pvc 1 mm thick was cramped between the angle-iron frames and held in front of the heater. The sheet first sagged and then tightened when the correct working temperature was reached. The hot malleable sheet was then pulled down on to the mould. Air evacuated through the peg board holes under the action of the pump forced the plastic sheet tightly over the mould. The fox was similarly formed over a fibre glass mould.

BXL Fromoplas high impact, rigid pvc sheet used to line the walls of passenger compartments in the BAC One Eleven short-haul jet. (Photograph by courtesy of Bakelite Xylonite Limited)

The design of this hexagonal expanded polystyrene box was evolved at Shell's Carrington Plastics Laboratories. It was originally conceived as a non-returnable container for short-haul transportation of tomatoes. (Photograph by courtesy of Shell Chemicals U.K. Limited)

These plastic strings, available in a range of colours, are made from Shell Chemicals polypropylene KZ 61-01 by Green Brothers Limited of Hailsham, Sussex. (Photograph by courtesy of Shell Chemicals U.K. Limited)

Hot wire cutter

This hot wire machine for cutting expanded polystyrene shapes can be home-made. In operation it will rapidly cut blocks of expanded polystyrene up to about 120 mm thick.

The upper drawing shows the construction of the machine as viewed from the rear when the top and back have been removed. The wiring between components is not shown on this diagram but is given in a separate wiring circuit drawing. The lower drawing shows the completed machine with top and back screwed in position.

The two ends, made from 18 mm blockboard, are glued and nailed together. A strip of wood is glued and screwed to one end to receive the aluminium bar. To bend the aluminium through a right angle, spread soap over the area of the bend and heat this area until the soap blackens. At this stage the bar will bend quite easily and through a smooth radius. A small tension spring is screwed to the end of the bar, and a crocodile clip is screwed to the spring. The spring and clip hold and tension the wire cutter. The bar can then be screwed to its wooden strip in the box.

A mains transformer is screwed to the base board. A suitable transformer would be one which reduces mains voltage to 12 volts on the output or secondary coil and capable of taking up to 48 watts. An output of 6 volts will be suitable if the bulb in the circuit is not included. A brass bracket to hold a crocodile clip is made and screwed to the base. This bracket is connected by insulated wire to the 12 volt transformer output via a car headlamp bulb holder. The other lead from the 12 volt output is screwed direct to the aluminium bar by one of the screws holding the bar to the box. The three mains leads — earth, neutral and live — from the primary coil of the transformer are connected — neutral direct to the neutral point of a 13 amp plug; live via a mains switch set in the front of the box to the live point of the plug; earth direct to the earth point of the plug. The top can now be screwed in place. This is

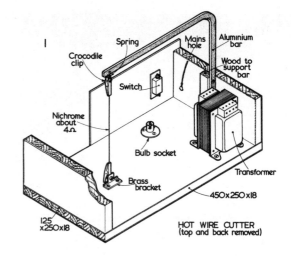

HOT WIRE CUTTER
(top and back removed)

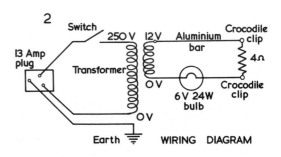

WIRING DIAGRAM

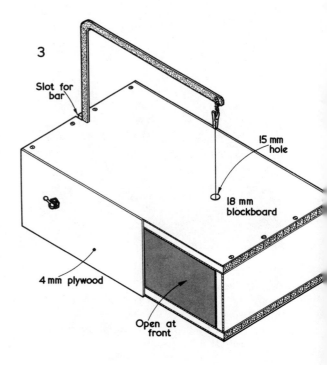

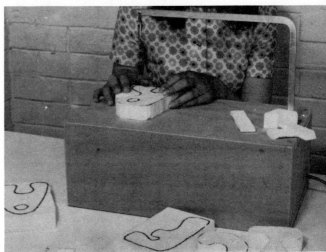

made from 18 mm blockboard with a slot cut at one end to receive the bar and a hole through which the cutter wire passes.

About 4 ohms of resistance wire is required, clipped between the crocodile clips. Eureka or Nichrome wire are suitable. A variety of car bulbs in the bulb holder can be tried until a reasonable heat is obtained in the resistance wire when the machine is switched on. The bulb gives a warning that the machine is on. The wire should heat to about 200°C to 250°C and must not run at red heat.

When this machine is in use particular care should be taken to ensure that the cutting wire does not overheat. If the wire becomes red hot, not only will the speed of cut be too fast to allow for accuracy when following lines of a shape, but styrene fumes will be generated. These fumes are irritating to the eyes and may cause dizziness and drowsiness, particularly in young children. The heat of the cutter wire can be altered by using a different wattage car bulb in the holder. Several different bulbs should be available to allow for changing. If the wire is running too hot try another bulb. The reasons for this are quite simple and can be worked out using the equation based on Ohm's Law —

$$\text{Volts } = \text{Amps} \times \text{Resistance.}$$

Shapes of all types may be cut in expanded polystyrene (EPS) with this machine. This white, light material is very easily obtained from waste packing. Do not confuse EPS with polystyrene, which is a hard plastic completely unsuitable for cutting by hot wire. One method of working is to cut templates from card, hardboard or plywood — animal shapes, scout or guide badges, tree shapes, leaves, Christmas tree decoration shapes. Then cut around the templates as they are held on top of the EPS in the machine. If templates are not available, shapes can be easily marked on to the EPS with felt pens. Display and name boards may be made by gluing letters and shapes on card, hardboard or plywood. These can be painted with emulsion paint. Quite large contour models can be built by shaping each contour level from EPS on the machine, gluing the layers together and filling the slopes between contours with plaster of Paris, 'Polyfilla' or 'Alabastine'. The resulting model land form can be painted to resemble the land it represents. EPS is very suitable for the bodies of model aeroplanes because the material is so light in weight. Interesting toys for young children can be made in the form of large jigsaws or shape puzzles for the children to fit together.

Dip coating with polythene

Powdered low density polythene, suitable for dip coating, can be purchased in a variety of colours – yellow, red, blue, green, black. The powders, being thermoplastic, can be melted on to metal surfaces using the methods described below. As a result of dip coating, metal articles are coated with a skin of polythene which is coloured, waterproof and a good electrical insulator.

Preparing metal for dip coating

Any of the metals used in hand craft work can be successfully dip coated. Their surfaces must be clean, completely free from scale caused by heating and free from oil or grease. The surfaces should preferably be cleaned with a medium grade emery cloth. Cleaning with emery cloth also provides a series of scratches which make a good 'key' for the skin of polythene. All sharp edges and corners must be removed. Sharp, angular corners will receive only a very thin skin of plastic compared with other surfaces when an article is dip coated.

Temperatures required

The article to be coated needs to be heated to a temperature of 300°C (570°F) preferably by being hung in an oven. The time needed to heat the metal will depend upon its size and shape. The article can be suspended from a shelf in the oven by a thin wire. A domestic cooking oven set to its hottest temperature is quite suitable. If working in a craft room a special oven may be employed. Alternatively the article can be heated by a blow lamp or over a gas ring, but the resulting temperatures obtained will only be a crude approximation of the necessary 300°C. Some practice will be necessary before being able to judge a reasonable temperature when using an open flame for heating.

If the article to be coated is of such a shape that there is a part which does not require to be dipped, that part can be held in pliers or tongs as it is taken from the oven. Usually, however, the piece can be trans-ferred from the oven to the polythene powder by holding its suspending wire in pliers.

Methods of dip coating

Several simple methods of coating can be employed. The easiest is to dip the heated article directly into the powder. Move the article about in the powder for about 10 seconds and then withdraw it. Knock off surplus powder by gently tapping the wire. Hang the dipped article on a nail or hook until cool. This method is quite satisfactory for small items without intricate shaping. A second method is to sprinkle powder on to the heated article. This method is suitable for flat pieces. A third method is to sprinkle a layer of powder on to cold metal and then place it into the oven. The plastic will melt on to the metal as both metal and powder heat up inside the oven. This method can be used when only one side of a sheet metal article is to be coated.

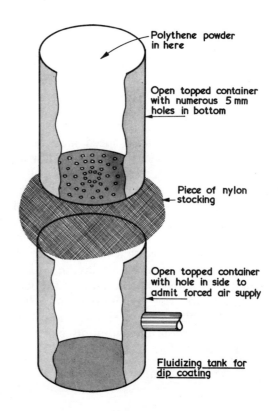

Polythene powder in here

Open topped container with numerous 5 mm holes in bottom

Piece of nylon stocking

Open topped container with hole in side to admit forced air supply

Fluidizing tank for dip coating

Fluidizing tank

To obtain the best results, producing an even thickness of plastic skin over all surfaces, the heated metal should be dipped into powder through which air is blown. Air passing rapidly through the powder causes it to be in a constant state of movement. The movement of the powder over the surfaces of the metal will ensure that all parts, including holes, crevices and other cut-away parts, are coated. Fluidizing tanks for dip coating may be purchased ready made, but a satisfactory tank for craft purposes can be made as described below.

Making a fluidizing tank

Obtain two large tin containers each capable of holding about 2 kilogrammes of powder. Large food 'tins' are suitable. The drawing shows how the two tins can be made into a fluidizing tank. The photograph shows the completed tank ready for use.

Cut the lids cleanly from the two tins. In the bottom of one, bore or punch a large number of 5 mm holes. Aim at a gap of about 10 mm between adjacent holes. In the side of the other tin cut a hole into which a short length of metal pipe can be soldered. The pipe should be of a size to which either the air pipe from a brazing torch or the pipe of a vacuum cleaner can be fitted. A rubber sleeve between the air supply and the pipe in the tin may be needed to make an air-tight join. If a vacuum cleaner is used the hose must be connected to blow air instead of sucking.

Open out the upper end of the lower tin to fit tightly over the lower end of the upper. This can be achieved by gently hammering lightly all round the inside of the lip of the lower tin. Join the upper tin to the lower by jamming one into the other with a piece of nylon stocking in between. The stocking allows a flow of air through its surface, prevents powder falling into the lower tin and assists in forming an air-tight seal between the two tins.

Place powder in the upper container, remembering that when air is forced through the powder its surface may rise by as much as 50 mm. Switch on the forced air supply. The air passing through the powder makes it appear as if it were a boiling fluid.

Using a fluidizing tank

Suspend the article to be coated by a piece of fine wire from a shelf in an oven. A single strand from a length of electric flex is suitable for this purpose. Leave the article in the oven at a temperature of 300°C (570°F) for as long as is necessary to heat the metal right through. Switch on the air supply to the fluidizing tank. Transfer the heated article from the oven to the fluidizing tank by the wire held in pliers. Suspend the article in the fluidizing powder for about 20 seconds. Remove, and tap the wire to knock off surplus powder. Hang the article on a nail or hook to cool. When quite cool remove the wire. Heat the flattened end of a strip of copper wire of about 3 mm diameter. Pick up some powder on the heated, flattened end. Work the resulting molten polythene into the area of the metal which was previously covered by the wire.

4 Acrylic Sheet

Acrylic materials can be purchased in sheets, in rods, in blocks and as powders. Of these, sheet is the most useful craft form. Various manufacturers make acrylic sheet under such trade names as 'Oroglas', 'Perspex', 'Plexiglas' and so on. Acrylics are thermo-plastic and can thus be readily shaped under the action of heat and pressure. Acrylic sheet is easily worked by hand with metalworking or woodworking tools. In this book the use of acrylics as a craft material is restricted to sawing, filing, drilling, bending, cementing and finishing sheet material to make up small articles of everyday use.

When purchased as new stock, acrylic sheet is coated on both sides with a protective layer of paper. This paper not only protects the polished surfaces of the sheet against damage, but provides an excellent surface on which shapes can be marked out in pencil or biro. Do not strip off the paper until as nearly the end of a job as is possible. This helps to retain the polished surfaces against possible work damage.

Working in acrylic sheet

Marking out

The straight edge of a ruler, a try square, compasses and other such marking tools will assist in marking out shapes in pencil on to the protective paper. When using sheet from which the protective paper has been stripped, a steel scribing point such as a metalworker's scriber or the steel point from a compass will mark the surface.

Cutting

Cutters such as that shown in Drawing 1 will make continuous straight cuts right along or right across a sheet of acrylic. The type of cutter shown is made by the manufacturers of 'Oroglas'. Four to six strokes of the cutter are necessary when cutting sheets up to 4 mm thick and six to ten for sheets up to 6 mm thick. The cutter does not cut right through the sheet but makes a deep scored line. Drawing 2 shows the method by which the piece which has been cut is broken clean from the sheet. Pressure applied with the palms of the hands and worked from one end of the cut to the other will break the sheet cleanly along the scored line. The freshly cut edges should be sanded with fine sandpaper.

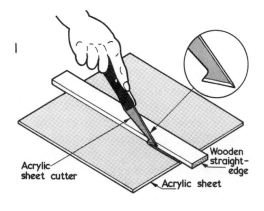

Acrylic sheet cutter
Wooden straight-edge
Acrylic sheet

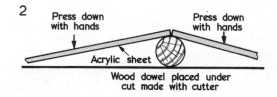

Press down with hands Press down with hands
Acrylic sheet
Wood dowel placed under cut made with cutter

Sawing

Cutters as described on the preceding page are only suitable when cuts are to be made right along or across a sheet. Other straight cuts will need to be sawn. A good saw for this purpose is a metalworker's hacksaw fitted with a blade of medium tooth size. Failing this a fine toothed woodworker's tenon or dovetail saw is suitable. Drawing 3 shows the relationship between tooth size and sheet thickness in a saw cut. If the teeth are over large, the saw teeth will jam against the upper edge of the saw cut. If too small, the task of sawing will be unnecessarily prolonged. When sawing with a hacksaw the sheet should preferably be held flat and quite firmly on to the top of a table or bench and held down under a straight piece of wood with a cramp such as a G cramp. When sawing take care to avoid slipping on the sheet's surface. Saw marks so made will be difficult to polish out. The lower the saw angle, within reason, the better will be the saw cut.

Quite intricate shapes can be cut in acrylic sheet with a jeweller's piercing saw on a piercing board. See Drawing 4. The sheet is held firmly on to the board and guided to the saw, which is worked up and down with the right hand. The board can be screwed permanently in position on to a bench top. Sawing by this method is slow. A fast cut cannot be made because of the danger of the thin saw blade heating the acrylic under the friction of its movement. The heating melts the acrylic and causes the saw to jam in its cut. However, this type of saw is valuable when intricate small shapes are required – such as when making jewellery parts in acrylic.

'Abro' tension files, which are designed for fitting into hacksaw frames, can be employed when making curved cuts in acrylic sheet. The sheet must be held in a vice. The 'Abrofile' is fitted into a hacksaw frame and the cut made as if the tension file were a hacksaw blade. See Drawing 5.

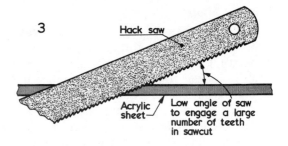

3 Hack saw
Acrylic sheet
Low angle of saw to engage a large number of teeth in sawcut

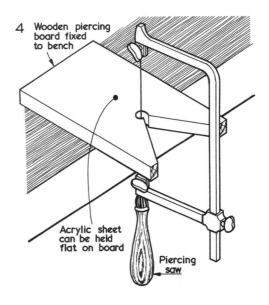

4 Wooden piercing board fixed to bench
Acrylic sheet can be held flat on board
Piercing saw

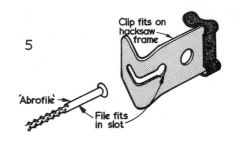

5 Clip fits on hacksaw frame
'Abrofile'
File fits in slot

Filing to Shape

Acrylic sheet can be filed using any grade of metalwork file. For rough shaping coarse (bastard) grades are suitable, and for the final finishing to shape before polishing smooth grades can be used.

A variety of lengths and shapes of files will be needed. Thus flat, half round, square, triangular and round files in a variety of lengths and grades should be at hand. A wire brush (file card) will brush out metal swarf from the teeth of files. Any pieces of metal remaining in the teeth will quickly damage the acrylic sheet.

Drawing 6 shows a suitable pair of loose vice jaws made from wood. These can be placed between the metal vice jaws to protect the acrylic from bruising by the metal jaws.

Material removed by filing can quickly damage polished surfaces of acrylic sheet. Blow such waste away from the work as it is formed.

Forming on moulds

Acrylic is thermoplastic. Thus sheets can be formed to shape after heating. Upon cooling the shape is retained. Because of this property, acrylic sheet can be worked to a variety of shapes on forming moulds. Heating of the sheet is best carried out in an oven. An ordinary domestic cooking oven is quite safe and suitable. In a workshop a small purpose-made oven might be considered to be better. When heating acrylic sheet for craft purposes, it should be placed in the oven on a piece of soft cloth resting on a flat surface. The temperature should be held at about 150°C (300°F) for approximately ten minutes for each 3 mm of thickness. The sheet will then be quite plastic and malleable. Soft cotton gloves should be worn when handling the hot sheets to avoid damage both to hands and the acrylic. Oven temperatures must not be allowed to rise too high. Above 160°C the sheet will become so soft that fingers may mark the surfaces. If very much above 160°C the plastic may degrade and give off fumes.

Drawing 7 shows a former made from wood. Its upper surface is covered with soft cloth to protect the acrylic.

Drawing 8 shows the same former in use. The heated acrylic is draped in position over the former. A second piece of cloth is then placed over the acrylic to hold it firmly in position until it has cooled. By pulling downwards on the wooden strips pressure can be maintained until cooling takes place.

Allow the cooling to take place slowly. Do not place in water or use a forced air draught to cool the heated acrylic.

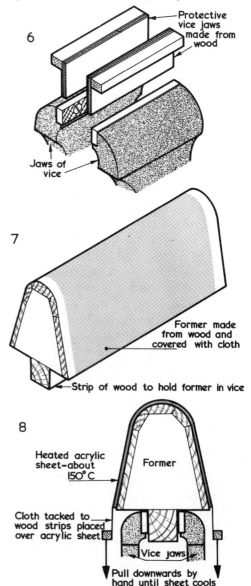

6 — Protective vice jaws made from wood

Jaws of vice

7 — Former made from wood and covered with cloth

Strip of wood to hold former in vice

8

Heated acrylic sheet—about 150°C

Former

Cloth tacked to wood strips placed over acrylic sheet

Vice jaws

Pull downwards by hand until sheet cools

24

Bending

Bending acrylic sheet through a small radius for such parts as box corners can be carried out if a narrow strip of the sheet along the path of the bend is heated to about 150°C. For this purpose a strip heater can be made. A very simple form of strip heater is shown in Drawing 9. A length of Nichrome (or Eureka) resistance wire is laid along a trough made from fireclay set in a piece of wood board. The fireclay when quite dry will be heat proof and also a good electrical insulator. Fireclay is forced into the groove in the wood whilst in its mouldable wet state. The trough is formed by pressing a greased piece of wooden dowel into the wet fireclay. A suitable voltage (12 volts) can be obtained from the transformer outlet of the hot wire cutter shown on page 18. The length and resistance of the Nichrome wire may be found by trial and error. When a sheet of acrylic is placed on to the strip heater, the heat from the resistance wire warms a strip along the acrylic. Warm both sides of the sheet, which will then bend very easily along the warmed area. To allow cooling without distortion, the angle of bend can be held in a jig such as shown in Drawing 10.

Drilling

In hand craftwork acrylic sheet can be satisfactorily drilled with a hand wheel brace and twist drills. Hand power drills can also be used. To prevent breaking out of the back surface of a hole, it is advisable to cramp the sheet being drilled on to a piece of waste wood. The drill will then pass cleanly through the acrylic and into the wood.

Always hold work to be drilled firmly in a vice or with cramps. If the work spins under the action of drilling, the polished surfaces of acrylic may be badly damaged.

Cementing

Acrylic sheets can be easily cemented together using such special cements as 'Tensol' (made by I.C.I.). Failing this an epoxy resin adhesive such as 'Araldite' will make very strong edge joints. The joints need to be held under pressure while the cement sets.

Finishing

High gloss polished surfaces are obtained by polishing with acrylic polishes. Metal polish is an excellent substitute. Remove marks with the finest wet and dry sandpaper before polishing.

Machine buffs, if used, must be clean. Saw marks on edges can be removed with a scraper honed to a straight smooth edge.

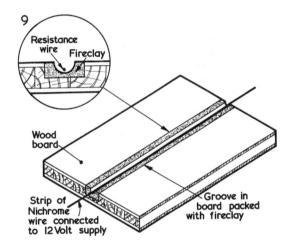

9

Resistance wire
Fireclay
Wood board
Strip of Nichrome wire connected to 12 Volt supply
Groove in board packed with fireclay

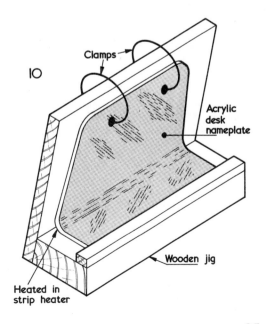

10

Clamps
Acrylic desk nameplate
Wooden jig
Heated in strip heater

5 Craft Work in Acrylic Sheet

Acrylic sheet can be obtained in a variety of colours, finishes and thicknesses. The most common is clear polished transparent sheet, but sheets in a variety of opaque and translucent colours are made, including black and white. Most are finished with both surfaces polished to a glass-like lustre. Other finishes – matt, grained or embossed – are also made. This variety of colours and thicknesses enables the hand craft worker to make a range of simple, flat, outline shapes in acrylic sheet – some examples are key ring fobs, name plates for attaching to suitcases, belt buckles. Small items of jewellery can also be suitably made in acrylic sheet, such as necklace parts, ear rings, hair slides, brooches. The metal pins and clips necessary for these jewellery items can be purchased ready made and glued to the acrylic with an epoxy resin such as 'Araldite'.

The outline of the keyhole plate has been marked in pencil on the protective paper. The sheet has been firmly cramped to the bench and a hacksaw is used to cut out the rectangle containing the plate.

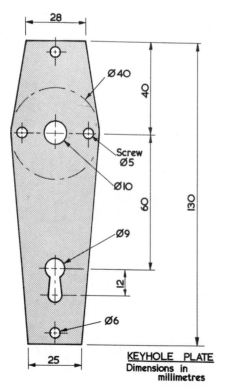

KEYHOLE PLATE
Dimensions in millimetres

Sanding the edge of the keyhole plate to a smooth finish prior to polishing. A strip of very fine grade wet and dry sandpaper is wrapped around a file and used to sand the edges.

Two such simple shapes are described – a keyhole plate for a door made from 4 mm thick white sheet and a neck pendant made from blue translucent 3 mm thick sheet. The shapes given for these two articles are only suggestions. Anyone making such pieces of work can easily think out new designs. Take a piece of paper and a pencil and sketch out ideas. From these sketches new designs will develop.

Making the shapes

The methods of working the two shapes are the same.

Marking

The outline of the shape is first marked in pencil on the protective paper covering the acrylic.

Sawing

The outline is sawn with a hacksaw or 'Abrofile'. The hacksaw is used for straight lines and the 'Abrofile' for curves. Shaped holes inside the outline, such as in the pendant shown in the photograph, are sawn with a piercing saw after drilling small holes through which the saw blade may be threaded.

Filing

Place the work in a vice, remembering to place the protective vice jaws in position, and file all edges, both inside and out, using suitably shaped files. Finish with the smoothest grade available.

Edge Finishing

Wrap sandpaper around each file in turn and sand all edges to a smooth finish. The best results are obtained by working the

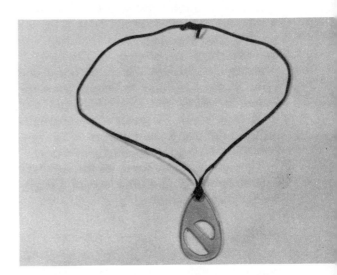

sandpaper along the edges with a 'draw-filing' action. Use the finest grade of sandpaper practicable.

Polishing

Apply acrylic polish (or metal polish) with a piece of clean rag and burnish the surfaces and edges to a polished finish. Several applications may be necessary if the sheet has been marked during working.

Neck chain

In the case of the pendant, thread a neck chain or leather thong through the suspension hole.

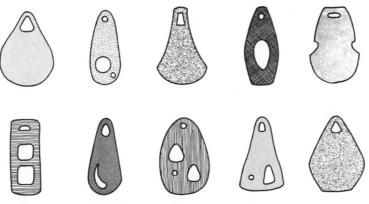

Some suggestions for shapes of pendants in acrylic sheet

A record rack

The making of this rack is a typical example of how a forming mould can be used to bend a sheet of acrylic to a shape after it has been heated to a suitable temperature. This rack was designed to hold twenty or thirty small records. The dimensions for the shapes of the flat sheet are shown in Drawing 1. Drawing 2 illustrates the shape of an end view of the rack and therefore gives the shape to which the forming mould will need to be made. A series of photographs on the next pages shows some of the processes involved when making the rack.

The acrylic sheet from which the rack was made was 3 mm thick and of a translucent purple colour.

Marking out

Commence by sawing out a square of the required overall size. Mark out in pencil on to the protective paper the shapes of the rectangular slots.

Cutting the slots

Several methods could have been employed to cut out the slots. They could have been completely sawn out with an 'Abrofile' held in a hacksaw frame or by sawing out with a piercing saw. Both these methods would have been rather slow. The method chosen was to first bore out a series of 4 mm diameter holes side by side to form a rough square in one end of each slot. At the other end of each slot bore holes only along the ends.

File the rough square holes to shape. Cramp the sheet on to a bench under a piece of wood. Thread a hacksaw blade through the squares and saw along the long edges of the slots. File these edges straight and sandpaper to a fine finish. Strip off the protective paper. If the sheet has become marked by holding in the vice or under the cramps, the marks can be sanded off with fine wet and dry sandpaper, using water if necessary. Polish the sheet with an acrylic polish.

Forming mould

Make the forming mould from wood. This can be of a quite rough, nailed construction providing the moulding surface is smoothly finished. Place a piece of soft cloth over the forming surface.

Shaping the acrylic sheet

Place the acrylic on to a piece of clean cloth resting on a flat piece of wood. Put into an oven heated to about 160°C (320°F) — about 10°C higher than the 150°C required to make the sheet malleable. Wearing gloves, take the sheet from the oven and drape it over the mould. Place a second piece of cloth over the moulding and pull the acrylic sheet to shape. Hold in position until cool. The rack is then finished.

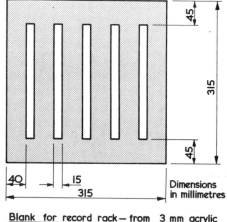

Blank for record rack — from 3 mm acrylic

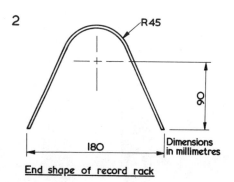

End shape of record rack

28

Drilling holes to form the cut out squares into which a hacksaw blade can be threaded. Note the waste wood under the sheet.

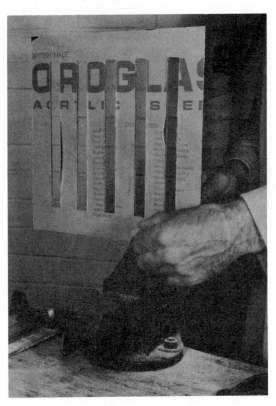

Completing the filing of the slots. Note the two larger files — one coarse, one smooth, which have been used along the long sides of the slots.

Filing the drilled holes to squares. A 150 mm flat smooth file is used. Protective vice jaws are in position.

Holding the heated acrylic sheet to its shape on the former. The upper piece of cloth is nailed to holding strips of wood.

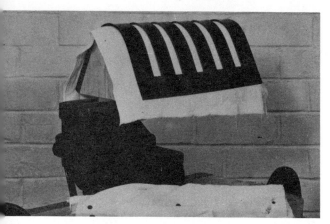

The completed rack resting on the forming mould.

Salad servers

Acrylic sheet, either clear transparent or coloured translucent is a very suitable material from which a pair of salad servers can be produced. Use sheet of 4 mm or 5 mm thickness.

Marking out

Make some preliminary pencil sketches on paper to explore the possibilities of different outline shapes. When a satisfactory outline has been drawn, copy it accurately full size on the paper protecting the acrylic sheet.

Shaping

Saw out the shape from the acrylic with an 'Abrofile' in a hacksaw frame. Use an ordinary hacksaw blade for any straight cuts. Place the sawn out piece in a vice and file it to its finished shape. Sand the edges to a smooth finish with fine sandpaper.

Assuming that the second of the pair of servers will be the same shape as the first, place the already shaped piece in position on the acrylic and mark around its outline in pencil. The second of the pair of servers can now be sawn out and filed to shape and sandpapered.

Forming the servers

Wrap strips of cloth around the handles of the two pieces and place them in an oven

to be heated to 150°C. Hold them at this temperature for ten or twelve minutes to ensure they are malleable, take them from the oven and press the spoon and fork ends between a pair of large serving spoons to form depressions. Now wrap the spoon and fork ends in strips of cloth. Reheat the servers and, when malleable, shape the handles. Allow to cool. Resist the temptation to plunge the hot pieces of acrylic into cold water.

Polishing

Polish all edges and polish out any blemishes with fine sandpaper and acrylic polish.

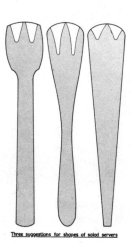

Three suggestions for shapes of salad servers

30

Draining rack

A plate rack made from 3 mm thick acrylic sheet is shown in Drawings 1 to 3. This rack is intended to hold wet plates while they dry after being washed. A coloured acrylic is possibly best.

Making the rack

1 Saw out a piece of 3 mm thick acrylic to a rectangle 280 mm by 180 mm.
2 Mark in pencil on the protective paper covering the sheet, the positions of the 20 hole centres at the bottoms of the slots.
3 Cramp the marked sheet firmly to a piece of backing wood and drill 2 mm diameter holes at each centre. Then drill each 2 mm hole with a 10 mm drill.
4 Mark in pencil the sloping lines of the slot edges. These should all slope at the same angle.
5 Saw down each slot side in turn while the work is held in a vice.
6 File each piece between the slots to semi-circular shape.
7 File and sand all slot edges to a smooth finish.
8 Heat each corner bend position in turn on a strip heater and bend to the angle shown in the drawings. Hold each side in position until the acrylic has cooled.

Magazine rack

The magazine rack shown in Drawing 4 can be made from 3 mm thick coloured acrylic sheet mounted on to polished wooden supports.

Making the rack

1 Saw out a piece of 3 mm thick coloured acrylic sheet to a rectangle of dimensions 390 mm by 300 mm.
2 File, sand and polish the four edges of the sheet.
3 Bend to the shape shown in Drawing 4, using a strip heater to heat the sheet along the bend lines. Take care when bending to make the sides as near right angles to the bottom as possible.

4 Make the wooden legs from 10 mm thick hardwood and shape slots in them to fit exactly around the acrylic half box.
5 Polish the legs and glue them to the acrylic, using an epoxy resin glue such as 'Araldite'.

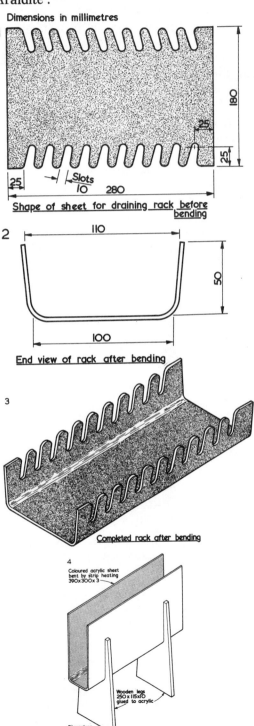

Dimensions in millimetres

1 Shape of sheet for draining rack before bending

2 End view of rack after bending

3 Completed rack after bending

4 Coloured acrylic sheet bent by strip heating 390 x 300 x 3
Wooden legs 250 x 115 x 10 glued to acrylic
Dimensions in millimetres
A Magazine rack

Motor cycle windscreen

The making of a motor cycle windscreen demonstrates how acrylic sheet may be bent to curves of a large radius without pressure being required above the moulding surface.

Drawing 5. A box framework is made from wood. The top edges of the box are shaped to the arc of the curve of the windscreen.

Drawing 6. Thin plywood is glued and nailed to the top edges of the frame to form a moulding surface on which the windscreen can be shaped. This mould surface should be covered with a piece of soft cloth.

Drawing 7. The sheet of clear transparent acrylic, ready shaped and made from sheet at least 3 mm thick is heated in an oven to 150°C and just placed on to the mould surface. The heated sheet drapes itself into the mould and conforms to its shape. Allow the acrylic to cool, when it can be lifted from the mould. Its various metal fittings can now be fitted to it ready to attach the screen to the motor cycle.

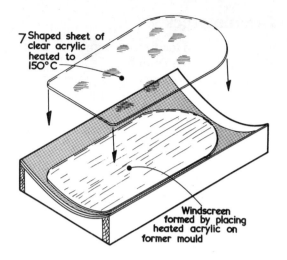

7 Shaped sheet of clear acrylic heated to 150°C

Windscreen formed by placing heated acrylic on former mould

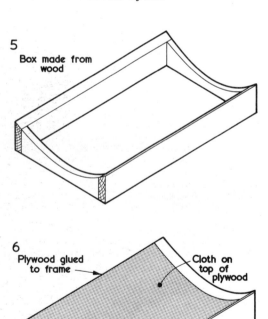

5 Box made from wood

6 Plywood glued to frame

Cloth on top of plywood

Completed former mould

Serviette rings

Strips of coloured acrylic sheet of 2 mm or 3 mm thickness can be bent to shape while hot around cylindrical formers. The rings so formed are suitable as serviette or napkin rings. The processes involved are as follows.

1   Obtain a suitably cylindrical surface around which the ring can be bent. Wooden or cardboard cylinders are suitable. The cylinder should be between 35 mm and 38 mm in diameter. The cylinder shown in a photograph below was made by wrapping paper around a broom handle.

2   Cut out the shape required for the ring from acrylic sheet. Four suggestions are shown in a drawing. File to the finished shape and polish the edges.

3   Place the forming cylinder firmly in a vice.

4   Heat the strip of acrylic to 150°C in an oven in order to make it malleable.

5   Hold the heated strip in a thick wad of cloth and wrap it tightly around the forming cylinder. Hold in place until the ring is quite cold.

6   The ring can now be slipped from the cylinder and is ready for use.

(right) Pendant made from blue acrylic sheet

(below) Small sherry tray in fibre glass inlaid with nylon dress material

(bottom left) Tea tray in fibre glass inlaid with grasses mounted in bronze gel-coat

(bottom right) Fibre glass lampshade mounted on a reading lamp stand

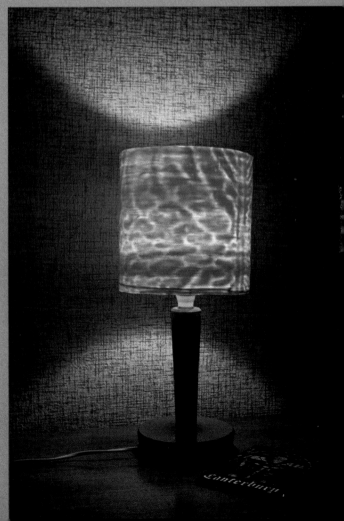

(right) Head in fibre glass taken from a mould from an original in clay

(below) Fibre glass canoe (see chapter 8)

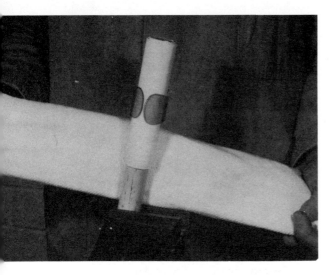

A forming cylinder made from paper wrapped around a broom handle. The holding cloth has just been unwrapped, leaving the completed ring on the former.

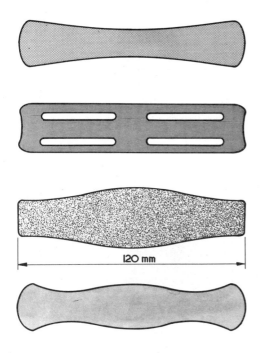

Some suggestions for shapes for serviette rings

A serviette ring from acrylic sheet made by the method described.

Box in acrylic sheet

This box was made in two contrasting colours from 3 mm thick acrylic sheet. The back, front, top and bottom were made from opaque black sheet and the two ends from opaque white sheet. The box did not require hinges because the lid pivots on two pins glued into the ends. Although made to a very simple design, careful working is necessary when making such a box if it is to function properly.

Making the box

All pieces except the pivot pieces can be cut from acrylic sheets by the method of scoring a line in one side and then breaking along the line across a dowel or across the edge of a bench. When cut out, all edges should be filed straight and flat with adjacent edges square to each other. The piece forming the body of the box should finish to 180 mm long by 150 mm wide. The piece for the lid should be 120 mm long by 149 mm wide. These dimensions allow for bending to the required shapes and for the lid to swing easily with a clearance of 1 mm between the box ends. The ends should be filed to finish 110 mm by 55 mm. The back edge of the box should be filed on a slope to allow the lid to swing between its pivots.

Bending of the box body and the lid is carried out using a home made strip heater. With the wire of the heater operating at red heat and by heating both sides along each bend line in turn, the right-angled corners can be quickly made. Once each bend has been formed it can be held in place by hand until the acrylic is cold – check that the angle is a right angle in each case.

The box body is then glued to the ends with an acrylic cement. An epoxy resin adhesive ('Araldite' for example) could equally well be used. While the adhesive is setting, the joints need to be held under pressure or under weights. While the glue is setting, saw out and file the two pivot pieces to shape and glue them into the corners of the angle of the lid.

When all the cemented joints have set quite firmly, place the lid in its position on the box. Bore a hole through each end and into the pivot pieces – 3 mm in diameter. Saw out and file to shape two tiny cylinders from a piece of black acrylic. These should be about 8 mm long and 3 mm in diameter. Glue the pins into the box ends so that they project into the pivot pieces on the lid. File and polish off any excess of the pins which project through the sides.

Finally polish all edges and polish out any blemishes, and the box is complete.

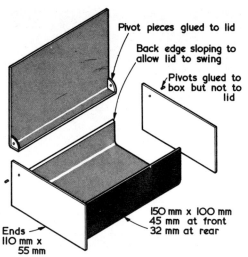

Pivot pieces glued to lid

Back edge sloping to allow lid to swing

Pivots glued to box but not to lid

150 mm x 100 mm
45 mm at front
32 mm at rear

Ends
110 mm x
55 mm

Exploded drawing of box showing construction

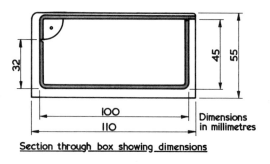

Dimensions in millimetres

Section through box showing dimensions

Cutting the pieces for the box using an 'Oroglas' acrylic sheet cutter.

Filing the edges of the piece for the body of the box. A 250 mm second-cut, flat file is being used for the purpose.

The base for a strip heater. A groove, cut in a piece of wood, is filled with fireclay. A channel is pressed into the fireclay with a greased length of wood dowel.

Gluing the ends to the box body. The second piece of wood will be positioned on top of the glued box to take a weight to provide pressure while the glue sets.

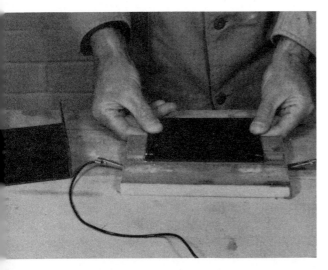

Heating along the line of the bend in the lid. Note the chalk marks to locate the line of bend. The coil for the heater was made from resistance wire wrapped around a nail. The nail was then withdrawn.

6 Introduction to Polyesters and Fibre Glass

Polyester resins

Polyester resins are thermosetting liquids which polymerize and so set to hard solids at normal room temperature without the application of pressure.

Other thermosetting plastics, supplied as powders or granules, require heat and pressure to cause them to polymerize and set. Because of the need to apply heat and pressure, articles made from most thermosetting plastics are restricted as to size. This restriction does not apply in the case of articles made from polyester resins and, with suitable reinforcement, very large mouldings can be made in this plastic. Articles made solely from polyester resins will be hard but are brittle, have low tensile strength and are not flexible. Such articles will fracture and break under an impact. When polyester resins are reinforced with suitable reinforcing materials, the resulting articles are not only hard, but also tough, strong and flexible, with very good tensile strength properties. Such reinforcing material can consist of paper, cardboard, metal wires or netting, hard polyurethane foam, man made fibre such as 'Terylene', carbon fibre and many other materials. The most important reinforcing material, however, is glass fibre, which accounts for the reinforcing of the vast majority of articles moulded from polyester resins. The term GRP – glass reinforced polyester, or glass reinforced plastic – is applied to mouldings made from glass fibres encased in polyester resin.

Apart from the very wide use in making GRP mouldings, polyester resins can be cast without reinforcement or can be used as surface coatings to other materials. Polyester resins are widely used in craft and art work and can be easily obtained in either large or small quantities. A list of suppliers will be found on pages 93 to 96.

Types of resin

A wide range of different resins can be purchased for a variety of applications. For craft work there are five main types of resin available, although others can be purchased.

1 *Gel coat resin* – supplied as a slightly thickened liquid for direct application to a mould. The first coat of resin applied when making a GRP moulding is the gel coat. Can be coloured with pigments or mixed with suitable fillers to give the moulded surface a coloured, metallic or other surface appearance.

2 *Lay-up resin* – general purpose resin for laminating glass fibre within a GRP moulding.

3 *Thixotropic resin* – a thick resin which can be applied to vertical surfaces without 'running'. Can be applied to the reinforcing framework of a sculpture form without falling out of shape.

4 *Clear resin* – water clear resin of a thin consistency for work which requires transparency in the moulded article.

5 *Casting resin* – for casting in solid blocks.

These resins are normally sold in a 'pre-activated' condition. In order to make them set solid, all that is required is to add small quantities of a 'catalyst' (hardener). Some special purpose resins are sold not pre-activated and require the addition of small quantities of an accelerator as well as a catalyst to enable the resin to set hard within a reasonable time.

Polyester resins will eventually set solid without the addition of catalyst or accelerator. Setting may take place after several months or after some years, depending upon the type of resin and the conditions under which the resin is stored.

Catalysts and accelerators

Catalysts and accelerators are added to polyester resins to initiate and control the time taken for the resin to set solid. The quantities which need to be added will vary between different makes of resin, and manufacturer's notes on such details need to be read with care. Variation in setting times from a few minutes to several hours after mixing can be obtained by the addition of suitable quantities of catalyst and accelerator. For most purposes there is no need to add accelerators to pre-activated resins.

Catalysts – sometimes referred to as 'hardeners', are usually peroxides and can be obtained either as liquids or as pastes. The liquid forms are more commonly used in craft work, being more convenient because of the ease with which small quantities can be measured. Paste catalysts are, however, easier to mix and disperse into the resins and, being more stable, can be stored for indefinite periods of time.

The word 'catalyst' is really wrongly used because the peroxide is broken up during the action of curing the resin. A true catalyst retains its original form while speeding up a chemical change. The word is, however, in general use in connection with polyester resins.

Accelerators – sometimes referred to as activators. Usually either cobalt salts or amines. Those supplied for craft work are mostly cobalt types. The accelerator speeds up the action of the catalyst. It must be remembered that catalysts and accelerators must not be mixed together before adding to a resin. *Such direct mixing can be explosive.*

After mixing the catalyst to a pre-activated resin the resin will set hard after a period of from several minutes to several hours depending upon the quantity of catalyst added. The resin does not fully polymerize (set or cure) until about a fortnight has elapsed. It is advisable to allow freshly moulded articles made in GRP to stand for a fortnight or so before being put into service.

Types of glass fibre

Glass fibre, which is drawn from molten glass to produce continuous filament, is the most often used reinforcement for polyester resins. The glass fibre filament is twisted into yarn, chopped into short lengths or left in filament lengths for 'rovings' to form the basis of several different types of glass fibre material. The most common types are:

1   *Chopped strand mat* – the yarn is chopped into lengths of strand each about 50 mm long. The strands are placed together at random to form a mat. The mat of strands is bonded together with a bonding agent which dissolves in polyester resin. Various thicknesses or weights of chopped strand mat can be purchased. This is the most common type of glass fibre material for reinforcing.

2   *Woven cloth* – glass yarn is twisted and woven into a cloth in a similar way to which other cloths are woven. Where flexibility is required, woven cloth glass fibre can be employed.

3   *Rovings* – continuous strands of glass filament are placed side by side. The strand is wound on to cardboard cylinders for easy manipulation.

4   *Tape* – twisted yarn is woven into lengths of tape of various widths, the most common being 50 mm wide. Edges and corners can be strengthened with glass fibre tape.

5   *Surfacing tissue* – thin sheet material placed on as a final laminate to hide fibre glass and to provide a reasonably smooth surface to a moulding.

These glass fibre materials can be easily cut to shape with scissors or with a sharp knife. When cutting with a knife work on to a sheet of hardboard. The knife must be sharp.

If a high strength moulding of good rigidity is required the ratio of glass fibre to polyester resin should be approximately 1 : 2.

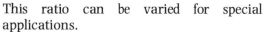

This ratio can be varied for special applications.

Glass fibre materials must be stored in dry conditions. Wet fibre glass makes weak mouldings which may delaminate or give rise to blisters.

Two photographs on this page, reproduced by courtesy of B.P. Chemicals International Limited, show the hull mould for a Royal Navy GRP minesweeper and the completed vessel being launched. The minehunter, almost entirely constructed from polyester resins and woven roving glass fibre, is believed to be the largest plastic vessel in the world.

The third photograph shows two rollers used in making GRP mouldings. One is a metal serrated roller, the second a mohair roller.

Moulds

The most common method of producing a GRP moulding is to build up layers of polyester resins and glass fibre on to moulds, using brushes and rollers. The resins are then allowed to harden on the mould. The mould may be male — the moulding is built up on the outer surface — or female — the moulding is laid up on the inside surface.

Moulds may be made from practically any solid materials at hand. The materials most frequently employed are wood, plaster, clay, fibre glass and various moulding rubbers.

The surface texture of a GRP moulding is an exact copy of the surface of the mould. Some care is therefore necessary when finishing the surfaces of moulds.

Parting agents

Polyester resins have a very strong affinity for many other materials and will adhere firmly to them when the resins have set. In some work the resins are employed as adhesives. If polyester resins are laid directly on to the surface of such materials as wood, fibre glass and plaster, the resulting mouldings cannot be parted from the moulds because they will have become glued together. There are some materials to which polyester resins will not adhere — some examples are polythene, paraffin wax and various moulding rubbers.

Materials to which the resins will not adhere are employed as 'parting agents' between mould and moulding. Two common parting agents are wax polish and polyvinyl alcohol (pva). The wax polish must not contain silicones. The pva is often supplied in liquid form.

Suppliers of the resins will also supply release agents. For general craft work wax polishes of the type used for polishing furniture or cars are suitable. When working with plaster of Paris moulds it is best to obtain the parting agents supplied by the resin manufacturers.

Colours

Colouring pigments can be freely used with polyester resins. The following types can be obtained from resin suppliers:

Pigments — either opaque or translucent.
Metal powders — copper, bronze, iron, aluminium to simulate metal surface finishes.
Other powders such as marble.

Tools

Few tools are required. Brushes and rollers are the most important. Purpose-made brushes for polyester resins are best. The bristles of ordinary paint brushes may work loose under the action of the resins. Flat rollers are valueless. Purpose-made serrated metal rollers or rollers made from mohair or lambswool must be used.

Sharp cutting knives are necessary. A palette knife is of value for mixing colours or for parting a moulding from its mould. A pair of wallpaper scissors is suitable for cutting glass fibre.

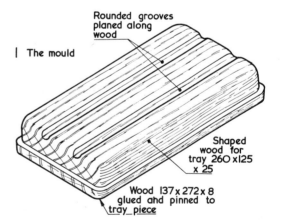

Rounded grooves planed along wood

The mould

Shaped wood for tray 260 x 125 x 25

Wood 137 x 272 x 8 glued and pinned to tray piece

This mould for a plant tray is made from two pieces of shaped wood glued and nailed together. All surface blemishes are filled in with woodfiller or plaster. The moulding surfaces are glasspapered to a fine, smooth finish.

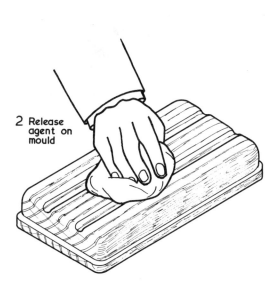

2 Release agent on mould

At least two coats of polyurethane varnish or paint are applied to the mould to seal its surfaces. Allow to set quite hard. After smoothing with fine glasspaper, the moulding surfaces are then wax polished.

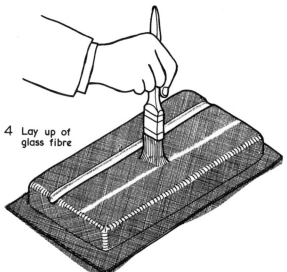

4 Lay up of glass fibre

Three layers of fibre glass — two of chopped strand mat followed by a layer of surfacing tissue — are applied. Each layer is wetted out with polyester resin applied by brush with a vertical stippling action.

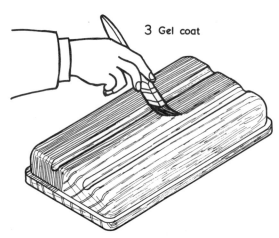

3 Gel coat

Pigmented gel coat resin is applied by brush to a thickness of about 1 mm. Use a purpose-made polyester resin brush about 25 mm wide. Clean the brush in cleaners after use. Allow the resin to gel.

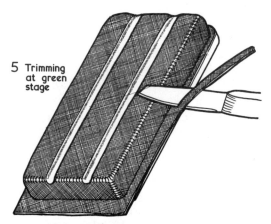

5 Trimming at green stage

After about 30 to 45 minutes have elapsed the laid-up fibre glass can be easily cut with a sharp knife. This is the 'green' stage. Too soon and the fibre glass will fracture; too late and the fibre glass will need sawing.

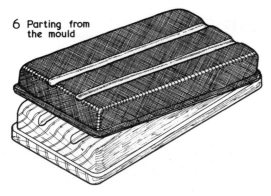

6 Parting from the mould

After a period of four or five hours the tray can be parted from the mould. A palette knife inserted between the mould and the tray can be of assistance for parting the tray.

This plastic garage door was made by Re-inforced Constructions (Leicester) Limited from B.P. Chemicals Cellobond polyester resins with glass fibre.
(Photograph by courtesy of B.P. Chemicals International Limited)

An abstract free floating form sculpted by Jean Gibson in polyester resin and clear Perspex. The clear Perspex gives a floating effect to the polyester forms.
(Photograph by courtesy of B.P. Chemicals International Limited)

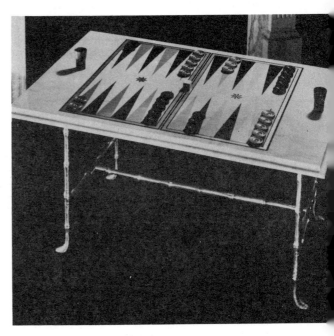

This backgammon table was manufactured by Tiberian Limited using B.P. Chemicals Cellobond polyester resin.
(Photograph by courtesy of B.P. Chemicals International Limited)

41

7 Craft Work in Fibre Glass

Fibre glass is well suited to the making of table mats. Not only is it a very tough, hard wearing material, but it is easily cleaned and will insulate a table top against the heat of such items as hot plates and tea and coffee pots.

The upper photograph shows a tea tray with four matching table mats made from fibre glass in which a decorative layer of printed nylon cloth has been laid. The decorative layer in such work can be any 'man-made' cloth of plastic fibres such as 'Terylene', 'Acrilan' or nylon. Cotton and other natural cloths are not so easily laid, being difficult to impregnate with resin. Paper can be used as a decorative medium providing it is well wetted with the resin. Coloured mats, either plain or decorated, can be produced by pigmenting the resins.

Mats may be of a variety of outline shapes — square, rectangular, circular, elliptical, hexagonal are examples.

Sheets of cellophane or cellulose acetate are used to obtain smooth surfaces on the top and bottom of the mats. Either of these two types of cellulose sheet will readily release from polyesters. The method of making this type of mat is shown in a drawing and in photographs.

Making a table mat

Preparation

The lay-up of these mats can be carried out as a continuous process without waiting at any stage for the resins to gel or set except when the lay-up is completed.

The following are required:
Sheets of cellophane or cellulose acetate cut larger than the mat size.
The decorative material — cloth or paper — cut ready to size.
Sufficient pieces of chopped strand mat cut to a size slightly larger than the finished table mat.

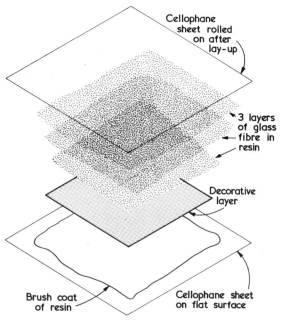

Cellophane sheet rolled on after lay-up

3 layers of glass fibre in resin

Decorative layer

Brush coat of resin

Cellophane sheet on flat surface

Lay-up resin and catalyst.
Container for mixing the resin.
Lay-up brush.
Roller.

The lay-up

1 Lay a sheet of cellophane on to a flat board. Fasten in position with drawing pins or Sellotape. Brush a thin layer of catalysed, unpigmented lay-up resin over the cellophane.

2 Place the decorative material in position on to the wet resin and wet it out completely with lay-up resin applied by brush.

3 Lay on three layers of chopped strand mat, wetting out each in turn with lay-up resin stippled in with a brush.

4 Place a sheet of cellophane on to the lay-up and roll it on with the roller. Work from the centre outwards to force out unwanted air bubbles.

5 Place the lay-up to one side to allow the resin to cure – two or three days.

6 When cured, peel off the cellophane from both sides. Saw and file the mat to its required shape. Finish the edges with fine sandpaper.

Four mats are shown in the lower photograph, each with a different decorative layer. Top left and bottom right are paper cut outs mounted on 'Acrilan' cloth. Top right is a piece of striped nylon cloth. Bottom left is a piece of patterned nylon dress cloth.

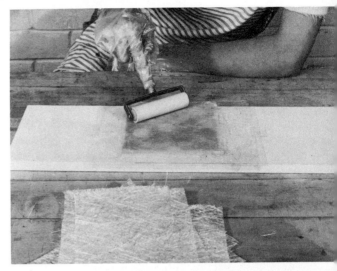

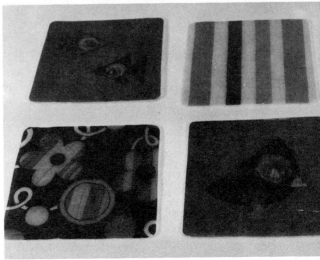

Stainless steel dishes as moulds

Fibre glass dishes can be made by taking mouldings from stainless steel dishes. This is possible because the outer surfaces of stainless steel ware are smooth and highly polished. These good moulding surfaces are repeated on the inside of the fibre glass mouldings taken from them. Only one layer of chopped strand mat is required unless the steel dish is large, when two layers may be necessary to obtain stiffness in the fibre glass moulding. The outer surfaces of the stainless steel dishes will not be damaged if wax release polish is thoroughly applied before the lay-up is started. The wax can be removed afterwards by washing the stainless steel dish in warm water and detergent.

The stainless steel articles in the examples shown here are used as male moulds. Other articles made from earthenware, china, plastics, other metals etc. may also be copied in fibre glass, but plaster, clay or fibre glass moulds will first need to be taken from the upper, or inner surfaces of such objects. The final fibre glass copy moulding can then be taken from the mould. Only one process is necessary when copying stainless steel articles. The double process of first taking a mould and then a fibre glass moulding from the mould is unnecessary. This is because the steel sheet is of an even thickness and thus the outer surface is, more or less, a replica of the upper, or inner surface.

Making the fibre glass dish

The drawings 1 to 5 are sectional diagrams through a stainless steel dish and through the fibre glass dish as it is laid in stages on the steel.

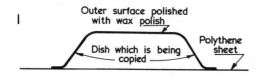

Thoroughly polish the outer surface of the

stainless steel dish with wax polish. Carry the polish over the edges and partly on to the upper surface. Make sure that the whole of the moulding surface is well polished.

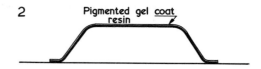

Mix up the required quantity of gel coat resin with the colouring matter to be used. In this case the gel coat was coloured by mixing an equal weight of flaked bronze into the resin. Catalyse the mixture and apply evenly over the moulding surface of the steel dish. When the gel coat has set it will adhere sufficiently to the polythene sheet to prevent the mould moving during subsequent laying of the fibre glass.

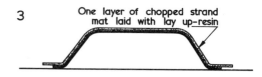

Mix lay-up resin with an equal amount by weight of flaked bronze and catalyse. Use this mixture to lay one layer of chopped strand mat over the gel coat. With a deep tray or dish the chopped strand mat will need to be cut into strips to enable even laying. Make sure that neighbouring strips overlap each other slightly. If colouring is used in the resins instead of flaked metal the more usual quantities of about 60 grammes of pigment to each kilogramme of resin should be mixed.

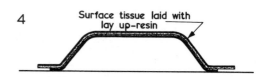

In a continuous process, directly the chopped strand mat has been laid, lay one

44

piece (not cut into strips) of surface tissue over the fibre glass. This should be laid with the same pigmented resin as for the chopped strand mat.

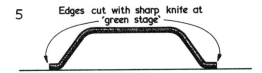

When the 'green stage' has been reached, peel the assembly from the polythene sheet and trim off excess fibre glass using a sharp knife.

Allow the fibre glass at least a day to cure, when it can be gently lifted from the mould with the aid of a blunt knife or a palette knife. The edges of the fibre glass will need to be sandpapered to a smooth surface and polished.

Two fibre glass dishes taken as mouldings from the outer surfaces of two stainless steel dishes. Top left – stainless steel nut dish. Top right – fibre glass dish taken from nut dish – metallic bronze finish obtained by adding flaked bronze to the resins. Bottom right – stainless steel tray. Bottom left – fibre glass tray taken from steel tray – bright yellow finish – yellow pigment added to the resins.

Fibre glass tea trays

Fibre glass trays with decorative surfaces can be laid up on moulds taken from existing tea trays or on moulds made from wood. The making of a male, wooden mould for a tea tray is the same as is described for the making of a plant tray mould on Page 40. The method shown here describes the making of a fibre glass mould from an existing tea tray. Any number of new fibre glass trays may be taken from such a mould. It is probably best to make a male mould – the new tray is laid up on its smooth, outer surface resulting in a smooth, upper surface on the tray. A tray may be laid up directly on an existing tray so that its under surface is smooth. This may be an advantage when a design is to be painted on its upper surface but it is not easy to obtain a smooth surface over the design.

The upper surfaces of trays made from male moulds can be decorated by several methods.

1   Pigmenting the gel coat with opaque colour or with flaked or powdered metals.

2   Laying a clear gel coat and painting a design with coloured resins on the coat when it has set. The design is then trapped between the gel coat and the first fibre glass layer.

3   Laying a printed polyester fabric such as 'Terylene' in resin between the gel coat and the first fibre glass layer. Such polyester fabrics are made from the thermoplastic polyester – not to be confused with polyester resins. Other man-made materials such as 'Acrilan' or nylon may be laid in resin. Natural fabrics such as cotton are best avoided for this purpose.

Making the mould

The drawings 1 to 3 are sectional diagrams taken through a fibre glass mould being laid on an existing fibre glass tray.

I Mould

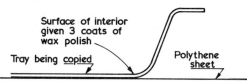

Surface of interior given 3 coats of wax polish

Tray being copied

Polythene sheet

Apply three good polished coats of a heavy, silicone-free wax polish to the tray's upper surface. Polish along all the edges and carry the polish partly over the underside near to the edges. If insufficient release wax is applied, the tray may be spoiled through the mould sticking to its surface.

2 Mould

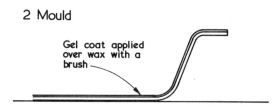

Gel coat applied over wax with a brush

Apply a generous coat of catalysed gel coat to the waxed surface. No pigment is required in this coat.

3 Mould

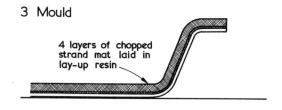

4 layers of chopped strand mat laid in lay-up resin

Lay up four layers of chopped strand mat wetting out each in turn with unpigmented lay-up resin. Lay the four layers in a continuous process, carrying on with the next directly the preceding layer has been wetted out. Roll each layer firm with a serrated roller. At the 'green stage' trim off excess fibre glass from the edges with a sharp knife.

When fully cured – several days – release the mould from the tray. Wash the tray in warm water and detergent to remove the release wax.

Making a new tray

Drawings 4 to 8 show in sectional diagrams the processes involved in making a new tray with its surface decorated with a printed 'Terylene' dress fabric. Such a tray is shown in the photograph.

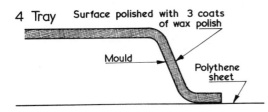

4 Tray — Surface polished with 3 coats of wax polish
Mould
Polythene sheet

Polish the working surface of the mould with three successive coats of wax polish. Place the mould on to a polythene sheet.

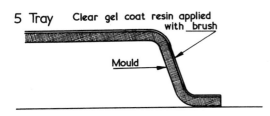

5 Tray — Clear gel coat resin applied with brush
Mould

Apply a catalysed gel coat to the moulding surface. In this case, in which a fabric is being laid on the gel coat, no colour is added to the resin.

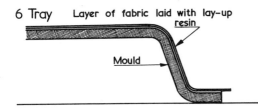

6 Tray — Layer of fabric laid with lay-up resin
Mould

When the gel coat resin has set, lay the fabric with a brush, using lay-up resin. No colouring is needed in the resin. The fabric must be laid with its outer surface on to the gel coat.

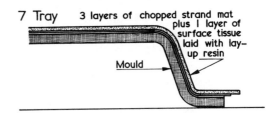

7 Tray — 3 layers of chopped strand mat plus 1 layer of surface tissue laid with lay-up resin
Mould

Apply three layers of chopped strand mat by brush with lay-up resin. No colouring is required. Add a final layer of surface tissue glass fibre with lay-up resin. The four layers should be laid in a continuous process.

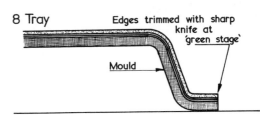

8 Tray — Edges trimmed with sharp knife at 'green stage'
Mould

At the 'green stage' trim off excess fibre glass from the edges of the tray. Failure to trim at the 'green stage' will result in much hard work later, when the excess can only be removed with hacksaw and files.

Allow to cure for at least a day. The tray should then release easily from the mould by slipping a palette knife between tray and mould.

Clean up the edges with glasspaper and polish with polyester polish.

The photographs on this and the opposite page illustrate stages in making a mould and in laying a tea tray on the mould.

The gel coat and four layers of chopped strand mat in lay-up resin have been laid on the existing tray. Note the polythene sheet under the mould protecting the bench top. The waste fibre glass will be trimmed with a knife at the 'green stage'.

A tray just released from its mould. The decorative surface of the tray was obtained by laying a piece of 'Terylene' fine dress fabric between the gel coat and the first layer of fibre glass.

The mould has been completed and allowed to cure. Applying release wax with a cloth. Note the brilliant sheen obtained on the surface of the mould.

(right) Statuette of a bull in fibre glass

(below left) Hawaiian girl carrying a fruit basket
– mosaic panel in polyester resins

(below right) Some examples of encapsulations

(right) Two small Christmas decorations made by pouring tinted polyester in the spaces of a ready purchased pair of plastic moulds

(below) Small translucent panel in polyesters and fibre glass

A stage in laying one of the layers of fibre glass. In this case, pigmented lay-up resin is being stippled on with a 50 mm brush to 'wet out' the glass fibre. Note the polythene sheet protecting the surface of the bench and the polythene glove worn by the girl. Polythene gloves protect the hands from the resin and from the fibre glass.

This tray was made with resins coloured with flaked bronze. Mounted over the coloured resin are some dried grasses which form a pleasing decorative spray. The order of working for this tray was to first brush a thin, clear gel coat on to the mould and set the grasses into its wet surface. When this had set, further gel coat resin was thinly brushed over the grasses. Then flaked bronze was mixed with lay-up resin which was used to lay three layers of chopped mat. Finally a layer of surface tissue was applied with the same coloured lay-up resin.

Lamp shades in fibre glass

Several different types of lamp shade can be made in fibre glass. Some of these are shown on page 51. The simplest method of making a lamp shade is to lay continuous glass rovings in polyester resin around a moulding cylinder. A jig for making cylindrical shades is shown below. This jig is easy to make and simple to operate.

Lamp shade jig

The moulding cylinder can be made from wood, from cardboard or from a length of heavy pvc piping. If made from cardboard or pvc, its ends will need to be plugged with wood. The ends of the cylinder are mounted in dowels set in one end of the wooden jig frame. At the opposite end is a length of dowel on which a roller of continuous glass rovings may be mounted.

Notes on release agents

If made from wood, the cylinder can be made with a slight taper towards one end to ease the problem of releasing the completed shade. Cardboard cylinders can be regarded as disposable, and if difficulty in releasing the shade is experienced, the cardboard can be torn from the inside in pieces. The best release agent is polyester film fixed to the cylinder with Sellotape. Failing this, the cylinder should be varnished and wax polished, or if pvc just wax polished. Polythene sheet can be used, but it tends to crumple and buckle when the polyester resin is brushed on.

Making a cylindrical shade

1   Paint catalysed gel coat resin on to the cylinder. No pigment need be added. Allow to set.
2   Mix a very small quantity of the desired shade of translucent pigment with lay-up resin. Catalyse the mixture. Feed the glass rovings on to the cylinder and lay on with the lay-up resin using a 25 mm brush. The cylinder is rotated as the lay-up continues.
3   When complete set aside for cure.

4   Allow about half a day and then release the shade from the cylinder. If a wire fitting is to be glued inside, this is the best time — if the fitting is tight it can be glued in with resin alone. If slack, some glass fibre may be added to strengthen the glue line.
5   Saw and file the top and bottom level and sandpaper the resulting edges.
6   Do not use the shade for several days. The heat from the lamp bulb inside a semi-cured shade can cause unpleasant fumes to be given off.
7   If a very clear shade is required clear resins should be used in place of lay-up resin.

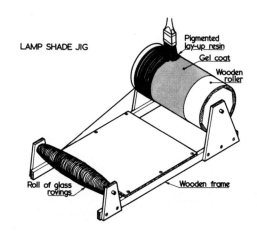

LAMP SHADE JIG

Pigmented lay-up resin

Gel coat

Wooden roller

Roll of glass rovings

Wooden frame

Examples of fibre glass shades

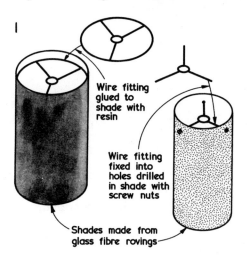

Wire fitting glued to shade with resin

Wire fitting fixed into holes drilled in shade with screw nuts

Shades made from glass fibre rovings

Two shades made on a lamp shade jig. The largest is 200 mm in diameter and was made on a wooden cylinder. It is fitted with a wire bulb socket holder glued in place with resin. Such wire fittings can be purchased ready made or made up from lengths of wire soldered together with hard solder. The smaller shade of about 140 mm diameter was made on a cardboard former. In this case the wire fitting is mounted in tiny holes drilled in the shade. The ends of the wires then have threads cut on them to take tiny screw nuts which hold the fitting in position.

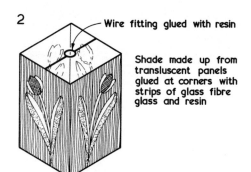

Wire fitting glued with resin

Shade made up from transluscent panels glued at corners with strips of glass fibre glass and resin

A shade made by gluing together translucent panels such as are described on page 67. These panels might be rectangular or made with sloping sides to form a pyramid type shape.

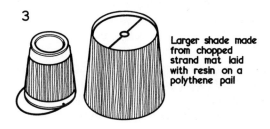

Larger shade made from chopped strand mat laid with resin on a polythene pail

Larger shades may be made up on polythene pails. They are best made from a single layer of chopped strand mat laid with tinted lay-up resin. The pail needs no release agent because polythene is readily self-releasing to polyester resin.

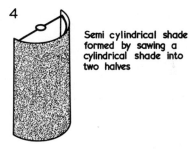

Semi cylindrical shade formed by sawing a cylindrical shade into two halves

A semi-cylindrical shade such as might be mounted against a wall light. Made by sawing a cylindrical shade into two halves when the fibre glass has fully cured.
Note: Any of these shades may be painted with designs worked by brush on the outside of the fibre glass, using tinted resins as the medium. Without such added decoration, however, the play of light through the glass fibre strands showing up in the tinted resins is very pleasing.

8 Making a Fibre Glass Canoe

The canoe described here was made on a set of fibre glass moulds supplied by Trylon Limited. Such a set of moulds is necessary when making a fibre glass canoe. Sets may be hired or purchased. See pages 93 to 96. Two refinements should be added when using this canoe in sea or 'white' water. Foot rests should be included, and the seat should be stiffened by connectors to the hull.

The processes involved in making the canoe are as follows:

1 *Preparation* – tables, trestles, glass fibre and templates, moulds, resins, catalyst, pigments, tools, cleaning fluids and rags, barrier cream, gloves.
2 *Release agent* – wax polish deck and hull moulds.
3 *Gel coat* – pigmented gel coat applied to deck and hull moulds.
4 *Fibre glass laminations* – lay up two coats of fibre glass.
5 *Jointing deck to hull* – bolt deck and hull moulds together and make the joint between the two parts.
6 *Release from moulds* – only when deck to hull joint has set quite firmly.
7 *Strip decoration* – decorative strip along joint line.
8 *The seat* – gel coat plus three layers of fibre glass. Can be made at the same time as the deck and hull.
9 *Fixing seat to canoe body* – fit and fix the seat into the cockpit.

A fibre glass canoe of this type can be the result of continuous working over a period of from six to ten hours. The work may, however, be spread over several days providing the joints between deck and hull and between seat and hull are roughened by scraping or filing before the joints are made. A typical schedule could be as follows:

Evening 1 – gel coat.
Evening 2 – lay up glass fibre on deck and hull.
Evening 3 – joint deck to hull.
Evening 4 – make seat.
Evening 5 – release body from moulds and fit and joint seat.

Materials, tools and equipment

To make one canoe 4·5 metres long the following materials will be required. The quantities quoted allow for about 20% waste.

Materials

Gel coat resin 5 kg   Lay-up resin 14 kg
Pigment paste ½ kg   Catalyst   ½ kg
Chopped strand mat glass fibre 40 g (1½ oz)
    15 sq. metres
Filler for fixing seat ½ kg

In addition the following should be available: Wax polish for release agent; cleaning fluid; barrier cream for hands.

Tools and equipment

50 mm brushes	50 mm paddle roller
Sharp knife	Large scissors
Some G cramps	Surform tool
Measure for resins	Catalyst dispenser

Containers for mixing resins and for holding cleansing fluid
Mixing sticks for mixing resins
Disposable polythene gloves or rubber gloves

Clean rags	Waste disposal bin
Strip of hardboard	Strip of wood

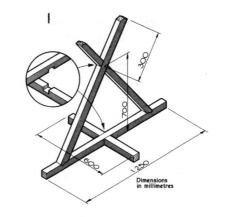

Preparation

If the task of making a fibre glass canoe is to proceed smoothly all materials, tools and equipment should be prepared and assembled ready to hand before commencing. The room in which the work is to take place must be well ventilated and sufficiently large to allow ample space for movement around the moulds as the deck and the hull are laid-up. There must also be space for a table or a working top on which materials, tools and equipment can be placed close to the work area. This table could be in a nearby, smaller room if necessary. The floor area under the moulds should be covered, preferably with a piece of 500 gauge polythene sheet. Drops of resin splashed from the work can be allowed to set on this sheet, when they can be easily peeled off.

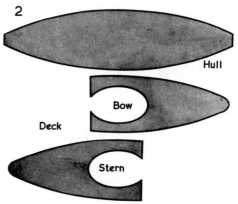

Trestles

Four purpose-made trestles as shown in Drawing 1 are needed to hold the canoe moulds firmly at a good, comfortable working height. The trestles can be made from lengths of 50 mm square softwood. The surfaces of the arms of the trestles on which the moulds rest should be padded with rags to prevent damage to the moulds.

Glass Fibre Templates

Cut out paper templates to the shapes required for the glass fibre mat. The templates may be made from sheets of newspaper placed against the insides of the moulds. Run a thumb over the newspaper along the top edges of the moulds to mark out the shapes of the required templates. The thumb marks a crease. Staple or Sellotape the sheets together, lift them out from the moulds and cut out the shapes with scissors. The approximate shapes of the three templates required are shown in Drawing 2. Two templates are shown for the deck and one for the hull. The deck templates overlap around the area of the seat aperture, so that when the fibre glass is in place three or four thicknesses will be laid-up in the area of the cockpit. This is where strength is needed.

Cutting the glass fibre

The templates are placed on the glass fibre chopped mat, and the mat is cut to shape around the templates with scissors. If scissors are not available for this purpose use a sharp knife. When a knife is used, a sheet of hardboard will be required on to which the cut can be made. Wear gloves when cutting glass fibre. Loose ends of the fibre can cause irritation to the hands. A

53

few snips cut inwards at intervals around the edges of each piece of shaped glass fibre will allow the material to fit more easily into the curve of the moulds as it is laid-up. When the glass fibre has been cut to the shapes of the templates to give two full length pieces for the hull and two of each of the bow and stern pieces, it will be found that there is a fair amount left over from the 15 square metres. This is required for strengthening the canoe and for making up the seat.

Checking of moulds

Inspect all the moulding surfaces of the three moulds. Carefully remove any specks of resin adhering to the surfaces, using a palette knife. Be careful not to scratch the surfaces. Tape over the grooves in the flange of the deck mould with self-adhesive tape. The taping of these grooves stops resin or glass fibre setting inside the grooves and so preventing good mating of the two moulds. The tape is removed before the moulds are fixed together after the hull and deck have been made.

Release agent

Polish the moulding surfaces and the flanges of hull and deck moulds with a wax polish. The polish chosen must not contain silicones. If the moulds are being used for the first time, at least three coats of the polish should be applied one after the other. If the moulds have been used before, one thorough polishing is all that is needed. The flanges of both moulds should be polished in addition to the moulding surfaces. Use natural rags when applying the wax or polishing and not rags containing man-made fibres. A high sheen should result from this polishing. Before proceeding to the next stage of applying a gel coat inspect the polished surfaces to ensure that no areas have been missed.

Gel coat

Apply a barrier cream to the hands.

Each person working on the canoe should be able to brush on about $1\frac{1}{2}$ kilogrammes of the gel coat resin before it commences gelling. Pour out sufficient $1\frac{1}{2}$ kilogramme batches of gel coat resin into suitable containers to enable both deck and hull to be coated. Mix into these batches the required colour pigment. A mix of 100 grammes to each $1\frac{1}{2}$ kilogramme batch will give a good, dense colour using opaque resin pigments. This is about 1 ounce to each pound. Take as many $1\frac{1}{2}$ kilogramme batches as can be worked at one time and add a measured amount of catalyst. This should be sufficient to allow gelling to take place in about 45 minutes. The quantity of catalyst required might vary between different makes of resin. Check this from the maker's instruction sheets. Directly the catalyst has been added the resin will commence polymerizing or setting.

Make sure that barrier cream is applied to the hands and allowed to dry. Brush a thick, even coat of the pigmented, catalysed gel coat resin over the moulding surfaces. Use 50 mm brushes. Do not allow the resin to form on the mould flanges. When one of the moulds has been coated, the second can be started. The next stage of laying-up fibre glass laminations can be commenced when the surface of the gel coat is tacky to the touch but when colour does not come away on the fingers.

Immediately the gel coat has been

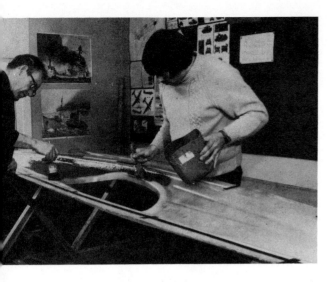

applied, clean out the brushes in cleaners and thoroughly wash them with hot water and soap. Put aside to dry.

Fibre glass laminations

When to commence laying-up

Directly the gel coat is tacky to the touch with the fingers coming away free of colour, laying-up of the glass fibre sheets can commence. If necessary, however, the lay-up stage can be delayed for a day or two. The gel coat will then still be tacky and will allow the laminations of glass fibre to adhere quite firmly. Two layers or laminations are required for this canoe.

Protection of hands

When laying-up fibre glass apply barrier cream to the hands, allow it to dry and also wear a pair of gloves. Either disposable polythene or household rubber gloves are suitable. The barrier cream will protect the hands against the resin and the gloves will prevent the glass fibres irritating the skin. Cleaning fluid and rags should be at hand to clean off resin from the gloves if necessary.

Preparing for the lay-up

The glass fibre chopped mat, previously cut to shape from templates, should be placed in a convenient position ready to hand.

Mix up lay-up resin in $1\frac{1}{2}$ kilogramme lots, one for each worker. Do not be tempted to work with more than this amount at any one time. Add the same colour pigment as was mixed into the gel coat resin, and add sufficient catalyst to the resin and pigment mix to allow a working time of about 45 minutes. If sufficient containers are available, mix up enough lay-up resin and pigment in $1\frac{1}{2}$ kilogramme batches for the whole job, but do not add the catalyst until each batch is to be used.

Laying-up: the first lamination

Brush coat a layer of the pigmented and catalysed resin over the whole of the area to be laid-up. If the hull is being worked this means the whole of the moulding surface. If the deck is being laid-up it means either the bow and cockpit or the stern and cockpit. Now place the shaped piece of fibre glass over the wet resin. Using a stippling action with the brush always held at right angles to the mould surface, work the resin into the glass fibre, adding more resin to the brush as the work proceeds. The stippling action forces air from between the glass fibre and the resin and eventually wets out the whole of the glass fibre sheet. A serrated paddle roller should also be used, once the glass fibre is all wetted. The roller assists in expelling trapped air and makes the lamination quite firm. Particular care is needed at the mould edges. Air trapped here between gel coat and glass fibre may be a cause of leaks in the completed canoe. The vertical edges surrounding the cockpit area also need to be firmly laid. When laying the glass fibre mat around the cockpit, some additional snips in the mat may be needed to work the mat around the curve of the cockpit. The deck is laid in two stages to each lamination. First the bow (say) is laid, followed by a stern piece. The hull, however, is laid in one long length.

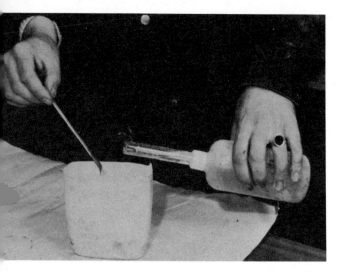

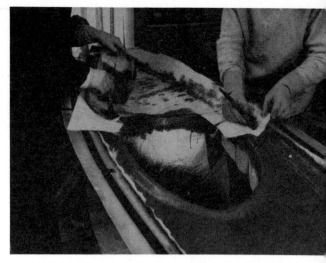

Laying-up: the second lamination

Immediately the first lamination has been laid, the second is commenced. It is laid in exactly the same manner as the first. The two laminations are therefore laid as a continuous process. Eventually both deck and hull moulds will be laid-up, each with two laminations.

Clean out brushes and rollers in cleaning fluid. Then wash them with soap and water.

Removing waste at the 'green' stage

Once laying-up of either mould is complete, a careful watch must be made to find when the 'green' stage has been reached. Prior to this stage the fibre glass will only cut with a breaking away of the cut edges. After the 'green' stage the fibre glass will require sawing and filing to remove waste. At the 'green' stage the waste can be easily, cleanly and quickly removed using a sharp knife. Failure to remove waste at this time will result in many hours' work sawing and filing once the 'green' stage has passed. Use a sharp knife, with the hand holding the waste well away from the knife edge. Take care not to damage or scratch the edges of the mould.

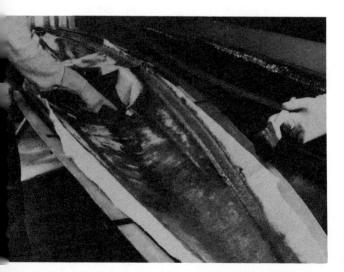

Jointing deck to hull

Strengthening strips

At the green stage, and before jointing the deck to the hull, it is as well to consider any strengthening strips which can be added to the canoe. A strip of chopped mat about 70 mm wide can be laminated along the inside of the hull at keel level to stiffen the canoe along its length. A wide band of chopped mat can be laminated across the inside of the hull at the widest part. This band should be up to 500 mm wide and will strengthen the canoe at the cockpit area. A strengthening strip should be laminated all round the cockpit edge to strengthen this vital area.

Timing

The ideal time to joint deck to hull is at the 'green stage', after the waste has been cut clear from the two halves. If this is not possible and a delay occurs, the deck and hull edges must be roughened. The last 30 or 40 mm of the inside of the two mouldings near to the edges must also be roughened. Scraping with a knife or roughening with a Surform tool are suitable methods. These areas will then present new faces which will adhere firmly to the resin applied to make the joint.

Preparation for jointing

Cut strips of glass fibre from the chopped mat material left over after cutting out hull and deck portions. The strips should be about 60 mm wide, in lengths each about a metre and of a total length sufficient to fix all around the joint line inside the mouldings. One lamination is sufficient to form a sound joint, but if two are thought necessary then twice the length of strip material will be needed.

Scrape or cut the jointing edges of deck and hull at a slight angle to form a shallow V when they are put together. Resin will flow into this V. See Drawing 2. Do not over-emphasize the slopes. Remove the self-adhesive tape from the grooves on the deck

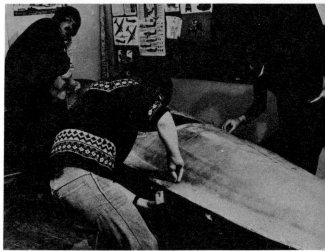

flange, and wax polish the area which had been covered by the tape. Check that all the flange surfaces are thoroughly wax polished.

Making the joint

Place the two mould cases together, deck upon hull. Check that they mate accurately. Bolt together with the bolts and wing nuts provided with the moulds. See Drawing 1. Place the whole mould case edge-wise on to a pair of trestles.

Strap a 50 mm brush to the end of a piece of wood which is sufficiently long to enable a person to brush resin along all the length of the jointing line while standing at the cockpit hole. Prepare some pigmented resin and catalyse it. Liberally brush the catalysed resin along the joint line on the inside of the canoe and also about 40 mm each side of the joint line. Take a length of the 60 mm strips of chopped mat, place it on to a piece of hardboard nearby and thoroughly wet the strip with the prepared resin. Drape the strip over the brush and wood and, working from the cockpit hole, place the wetted strip over and along the joint line by inverting the wood. The strip will sink into position but should be assisted by stippling with the elongated brush. Repeat this until the canoe is jointed one side. Allow the resin on that side to commence setting, turn over the canoe within

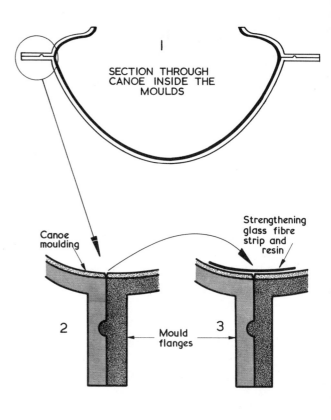

1 SECTION THROUGH CANOE INSIDE THE MOULDS

Canoe moulding

Strengthening glass fibre strip and resin

2

3

Mould flanges

its moulds and in a similar manner joint the other side. See Drawing 3. Two strips can be laid over the joint line if thought necessary.

It is advisable to tie a piece of cloth over the head and hair while making the joint. Resin caught in the hair is quite difficult to remove once it has set.

Release from moulds

Do not risk releasing the canoe shell from the moulds for at least 24 hours. This will give time for the joint line resin to set firmly. Remember however that full polymerization will not be complete for another week or so.

Parting from moulds

First unscrew the wing nuts and remove the bolts holding the two mould cases together. Run a palette knife around and between the flanges to break the seal between them. Push thin wooden wedges between the flanges in several places around the moulds. The deck mould should part from the canoe shell as the wedges are gently pushed forwards. As parts of the mould release from the shell air patches can be quite clearly seen as they form between the two surfaces. Judicious thumping with the palms of the hands will spread the releasing area if any difficulty is encountered. Hitting the mould with a piece of wood or with a hammer or mallet will almost certainly damage and fracture the moulds. After releasing the deck mould, place the hull, still in its mould, on to the floor. Two people pressing gently downwards and around the flanges will effectively release the hull. Be careful of the 'flashings' protruding around the joint line. These are quite sharp and can cause severe cuts.

Removal of flashing

Place the canoe shell on to a pair of well padded trestles and file off the flashing with a Surform tool or file. Fill in any gaps along the joint line with pigmented and catalyzed resin to which some calcium carbonate

(chalk) filler has been added. When this sets, clean up around the joint line with glass-paper.

Strip decoration

Self-adhesive waterproof tape can be fixed all around the canoe over the joint line. Although not necessary, this strip makes a pleasing decorative line around the canoe.

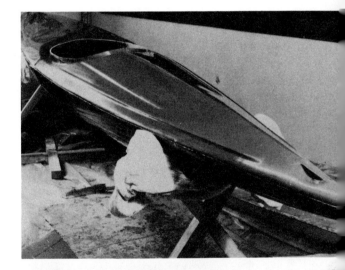

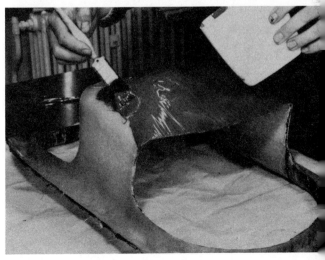

The seat

The same procedure is adopted when making the seat as when making the canoe shell. First wax polish the mould, then apply a gel coat, followed by laminating three layers of chopped strand mat to be trimmed at the 'green' stage. After 24 hours have elapsed release the seat from its mould. The important difference when making the seat is that the chopped strand mat is applied as small pieces overlapping each other. This is necessary because the seat is a much more complex shape than either the deck or the hull. The remaining waste from the original length of chopped strand mat can be used for making the seat.

Fixing the seat

The opening in the deck may need adjusting slightly by filing with a Surform tool to ensure the seat combing fits snugly in place. If both deck and seat edges have been cleanly cut to the mould edges at the 'green' stage, this fitting will not take up much time. Once fitted, the seat is cramped to the deck with G cramps over paddings of waste rag. The pads will prevent damage to the glossy surfaces of the canoe. The cramps need only be tightened sufficiently to keep the seat in place while it is glued.

Gluing seat to canoe

Place the canoe upside down on to a pair of well padded trestles. This enables a person kneeling on the floor to work with his head inside the cockpit. Make up a paste of about 250 grammes of lay-up resin, pieces of chopped strand mat and some calcium carbonate filler. This should make a paste somewhat like putty. Add pigment and catalyst. The mixture is applied with a palette knife from inside the cockpit. It is squeezed into the spaces between the seat surround and the cockpit edge. Then turn the canoe upright again and work the putty-like mixture around the outside between the seat and deck. At the 'green' stage trim off any excess with a sharp knife.

Remove the G cramps and finish off the joint to a smooth surface, using a second paste consisting of resin, calcium carbonate, pigment and catalyst.

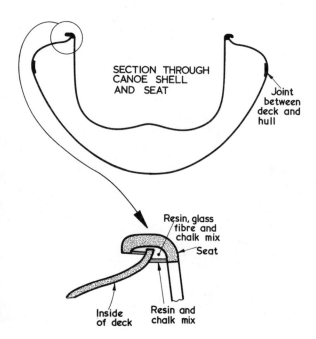

SECTION THROUGH CANOE SHELL AND SEAT

Joint between deck and hull

Resin, glass fibre and chalk mix

Seat

Inside of deck

Resin and chalk mix

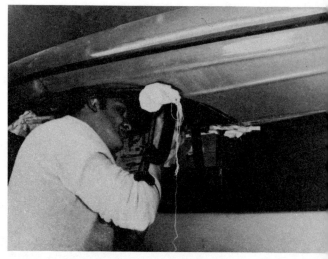

9 Craft Work in Polyester Resins

Encapsulation

The enclosing of articles within clear polyester resins is a simple operation, and very good results can be achieved if sufficient care is taken when making the encapsulation. The encapsulation may be for decorative purposes – brooches, rings, pendants, paper weights and lamp bases being examples – or may be for the preservation of biological specimens such as insects, butterflies, moths, small skeletons, flowers and seed heads. Polyester resins for encasing such items are sold as clear casting resins and are formulated especially for the purpose.

Notes on clear casting resins

1   Most resins sold for craft use are pre-activated – normally by the addition of about 2% of cobalt activator. Such resins are discoloured by the activator and are usually slightly pink in colour. Pre-activated clear casting resins contain no more than 0·5% of activator in order to avoid this discolouration. Because of the small amount of added activator, the usual 30 minutes to 40 minutes of setting time common to pre-activated resins is greatly extended when using clear casting resins.

2   Complete polymerization and hence cure of activated, catalysed resins will not take place in the presence of oxygen. This explains why the surfaces of cured gel coat resins are always slightly tacky. In the presence of the oxygen in the air the molecules on the surface of the cured gel coat cannot fully polymerize. To prevent this occurring, most resins, such as lay-up resins, have small quantities of wax added. In use, the wax floats to the surface of a lay-up. The wax effectively prevents the surface molecules of the resin coming into contact with the air. This allows full surface cure of the resin.

The addition of this small quantity of wax, however, causes the resins to appear slightly opaque. To avoid this cloudiness no wax is added to clear casting resins. Because of this, surfaces of clear casting resins which are exposed to the air remain tacky after the resin has cured. This tackiness can be avoided by rolling polyester film on to the exposed surfaces when gelling of the resin commences. The film excludes the air and the full polymerization and thus cure of the surfaces can take place.

3   Resins which are pre-activated with the usual amount of 2% of activator will commence gelling within 30 to 40 minutes after the addition of the usual 2% of catalyst. If such resins are poured to form castings of any volume, considerable shrinking will take place as curing progresses. Much heat will also be generated by the exothermic action of the fairly rapid polymerization. The heat and shrinking will cause splits, cracks and hollows to form within and on the surfaces of the casting. Such splitting and cracking is reduced to a minimum when clear casting resins are used. This is because of the slowness of the polymerization due to the small percentage of activator within the resins. If large castings are required the time of polymerization can be further increased by adding less than the usual 2% of catalyst.

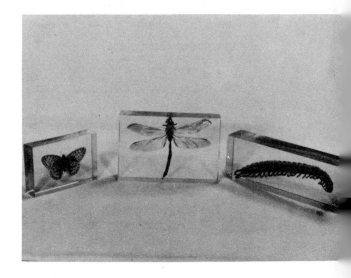

Method of making an encapsulation

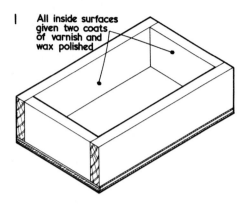

I All inside surfaces given two coats of varnish and wax polished

The drawing shows a casting box made from pieces of wood nailed together. Before joining the box sides and bottom together, each piece should be varnished and wax polished to a smooth surface. No slope is required on the box sides – the shrinking which takes place as the resin sets will ensure that the casting will release fairly easily from the box, perhaps assisted by a tap or two on the outside of the box. The varnishing and wax polishing must be thorough – any part of the wood not covered will adhere quite firmly to the resin and so prevent removal of the casting.

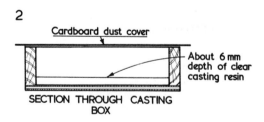

2

Cardboard dust cover

About 6 mm depth of clear casting resin

SECTION THROUGH CASTING BOX

First stage of casting

Mix sufficient clear casting resin with 2% of catalyst to form a layer about 6 mm deep in the bottom of the casting box. Pour the catalysed resin into the box. Stand to one side with a piece of cardboard covering the mouth of the box. The cardboard will prevent dust settling on the surface of the resin. Any air bubbles in the resin should rise to the surface and break.

3

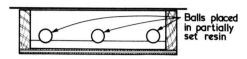

Balls placed in partially set resin

Second stage of casting

Allow the resin to gel partially. This will take perhaps two hours, because of the low activator content of the resin. At this partial gel stage the required number of glass balls can be placed on the resin and pushed slightly below the surface as shown in the sectional drawing. Place the box to one side, with its cardboard cover replaced, for several hours until the resin has set. Overnight would be a convenient length of time.

The photograph shows a decorative encapsulation made by casting clear polyester resin into a casting box around a collection of glass Christmas tree balls. The balls are placed in the resin in two layers. This encapsulation measures about 100 mm by 60 mm by 30 mm and is used as a windowsill decorative piece. As it stands on the sill on a bright day the sun shines through the clear resin and catches on the colours of the glass balls which are reflected back into the optically clear resin.

The making of this decorative item is typical of the general method of encapsulating objects in polyester resin.

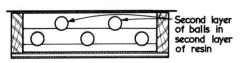

4

Second layer of balls in second layer of resin

Third stage of casting

Mix up sufficient clear resin with 2% of catalyst to cover the layer of glass balls. When this second layer has partially set place the second layer of glass balls in position and again place the box aside to allow the resin of the second layer to set. It should be noted that the surface of the first layer is still tacky due to the lack of wax in the resin. This means that the two layers will adhere to each other quite firmly.

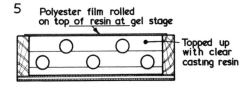

5

Polyester film rolled on top of resin at gel stage

Topped up with clear casting resin

Fourth stage of casting

Mix and pour a third layer of catalysed resin to fill the box. Allow gelling to commence — perhaps two hours after pouring. At gel stage roll a piece of polyester film on to the top surface to allow the upper surface to polymerize fully in the absence of air caused by the contact with the film.

Allow the casting to remain in its box for a further two days or so, when the polyester film can be peeled from the top — it can be used again if required on another casting. The mould should now come free from the casting box — a gentle tap or two on the outside of the box may be necessary.

If the polyester film has been laid without trapping air bubbles, the upper surface of the casting should be smooth and glass-like. It may be necessary to sandpaper and polish this surface either if polyester film has not been used or if the surface is not smooth because of trapped air bubbles.

The layers of resin can be seen in such a casting but are not obtrusive in any way. If thought necessary, every surface of the block can be sandpapered and polished as described on page 64.

Some points to note

A coloured base can easily be formed on any encapsulation by mixing opaque pigment with the final layer poured into the casting box. The surface of this layer need not be covered with polyester film. It can easily be sandpapered when fully cured. Any colour can be used.

When placing items in a casting, care must be taken not to trap air bubbles as these are unsightly. After pouring the first layer, which is then allowed to set, a small quantity of resin can be poured into which the specimen is placed. If it is positioned and then moved about from side to side with the aid of tweezers, air bubbles can be worked out from below. The second layer can then be poured on to the specimen.

A small quantity — a drop or two — of translucent pigment can be added to clear casting resin to tint the casting. A speck of opaque pigment can also be used for this purpose, but a little goes a very long way in tinting castings.

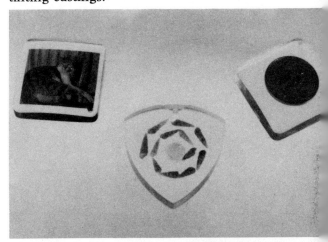

The photograph shows three small encapsulations each measuring about 35 mm by 35 mm by 6 mm. The top left is a 35 mm Agfacolor transparency film of a favourite cat. The top right is a penny piece trapped in polyester and the lower photograph shows a group of tiny sea shells arranged around a central shell in a spiral. These encapsulations were made in prepared polythene moulds supplied by Bondaglas-Voss. Each was made in two stages, the items each being placed between two layers of resin.

The photographs on this page show some of the stages in the making of an encapsulation. In this example the mould box was a rectangular polythene box with highly polished interior surfaces.

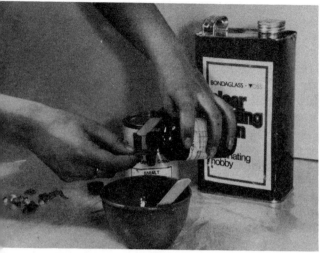

Pouring a measured quantity of catalyst for mixing with the resin. In this case a polythene dispenser is used to measure out the exact amount of required catalyst into a previously measured quantity of resin — in this case 60 grammes of resin.

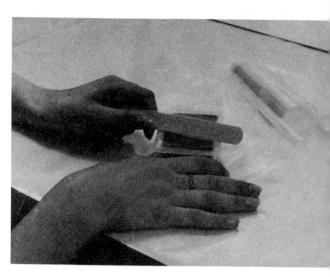

Rubbing down polyester film on to the gelled surface of the top layer of the casting.

This particular encapsulation was polished on all six surfaces. First a flat surface was achieved by rubbing down on to very smooth wet and dry sandpaper. This smooth surface was then polished with metal polish. Special polyester polishes achieve excellent results quicker than will metal polish but, in the absence of polyester polishes, metal polish can be used to produce good glassy surfaces.

The rubbing down and polishing of this item was only necessary in order to reduce its size. The polythene moulds made for encapsulating produce excellent surfaces on the casting which do not usually need to be polished.

Placing the parts of the design in position on the first layer of resin. The first layer has set and about 2 mm depth of catalysed resin has been poured on top of the first layer. Into this 2 mm depth of resin the various pieces are being placed using a pair of watchmaker's tweezers for positioning.

Mosaic panels in polyester resins

Opaque or translucent mosaics may be made in polyester resins. Small coloured pieces (the 'tesserae') are made from either opaque or translucent pigmented resins. The opaque tesserae can be mounted in resin on chipboard, the translucent tesserae can be mounted in resin on a sheet of glass fibre reinforced resin.

Making the tesserae

Drawing 1. Polish one side of a sheet of glass with silicone-free wax polish. Form a series of shallow recesses on the polished surface by sticking masking tape around the edges and dividing the sheet into as many compartments as are required with strips of 'Plasticine'.

Drawing 2. Place the glass on a table and check that it is level with a spirit level. Mix up small quantities of resin and pigments in separate containers. Catalyse the resin mixtures and pour them separately into the shallow recesses to a thickness of about 4 mm. Each recess should contain a different colour.

Drawing 3. When the resin has gelled — about 30 minutes — and before it sets hard, cut through the sheets of resin with a sharp knife to form the various shapes required for the tesserae. These may be square, rectangular or any other shape as thought fit. Leave the pieces to set hard, when they can then be easily parted from the polished glass.

Making an opaque mosaic

Spread a thin layer of pigmented, catalysed resin over the back of a chipboard panel and allow it to set hard. This backing resin will balance the mosaic on the face side of the board and prevent the board distorting. Mix some resin with the desired background colour pigment and spread it over part of the face of the panel. While the resin is wet place the tesserae into position to form the desired mosaic. Spread only that area of background which can be worked before the resin gels. The mosaic can easily be laid in small areas

at a time. When the mosaic pattern has been completed, allow the resin to gel. Then tape the edges of the board with masking tape to form a shallow field all around the panel. Level up the board with a spirit level and gently pour pigmented catalysed resin into the spaces between the tesserae. Place aside to harden.

Making a translucent mosaic

Make up a panel from a single thickness of chopped strand mat in clear resin on a sheet of polished glass. Allow to harden. Mount translucent tesserae on to this panel in a similar manner to that in which the opaque tesserae are mounted on chipboard, using translucent pigment in the background resin.

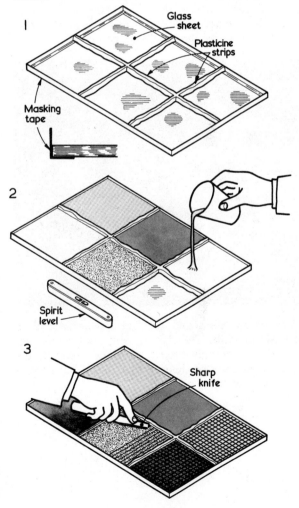

Glass sheet

Plasticine strips

Masking tape

Spirit level

Sharp knife

Six different colours of resin have been poured into recesses formed by 'Plasticine' strips on the polished surface of a sheet of glass — red, yellow, blue, black, green and orange. Waiting for gelling of the resin to commence.

Cutting the gelled resin into tesserae with a sharp knife. The cutting must be carried out just at the right time. If the resin is too soft, the cut will not be clean. If the resin is too hard, it will not cut at all.

A completed opaque mosaic worked on to a sheet of 18 mm thick chipboard. The coloured tesserae have been set in a background of white pigmented resin.

Note: If a sheet of polished glass separated into recesses is kept at hand when working in coloured resin, any resin remaining from other work can be poured to form mosaic pieces which can be used when the need arises.

Translucent decorative fibre glass panels

Translucent panels can be made from glass fibre and polyester resins for fitting into doors or windows as decorative features or made in sets for joining together to make lamp shades. The method of working shown here makes use of a mould made from paraffin wax. A fibre glass backing panel is formed on the wax mould. The backing panel can be laid-up on moulds made from 3 mm thick polythene sheet. The processes involved when using a thick polythene sheet mould are the same as those involved when using a paraffin wax mould. When the required design has been carved with a lino tool on the thick polythene sheet, the mould can be used many times over to produce a large number of identical translucent panel backings. The polythene sheet, however, cannot be re-used for another design. Only a few panel backings may be taken from a paraffin wax mould, but the wax may be remelted to form a new mould for another design. A wax mould is therefore cheaper to make than a polythene mould. If many identical panels are required polythene sheet moulds are to be preferred. No release agents are required for either paraffin wax or polythene sheet as both are self-releasing to polyester resins.

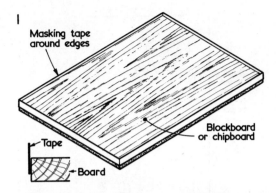

Saw a piece of blockboard or chipboard to a size large enough to take the required panel. Plane its edges straight and square. Apply masking tape along each edge as shown. The tape should stand proud of the board's surface by about 8 mm to leave a field into which molten paraffin wax may be poured.

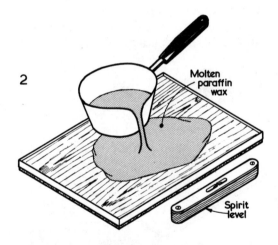

Cut up sufficient paraffin wax into small pieces and place in a saucepan or similar container. There is a fire danger if candle wax is exposed to heat such as from a gas ring. To avoid this danger place the saucepan in a larger vessel which contains boiling water. The wax will gradually melt to a liquid ready for pouring. Pour the wax quickly and evenly on to the board to form an even thickness of between 3 mm and 5 mm. The moulding box should be levelled with a spirit level before pouring to ensure consistent thickness of wax.

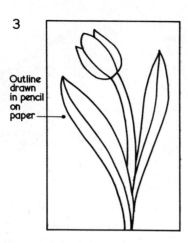

3

Outline drawn in pencil on paper

While the wax is cooling and setting, draw the required design in pencil on a piece of paper. This should be a full size drawing from which the mould can be copied. The design should contain a closed area for each coloured portion. This allows each area of coloured resin to be poured without running into neighbouring areas of different colours. The only area which should be continuous is the background, if any, of the design.

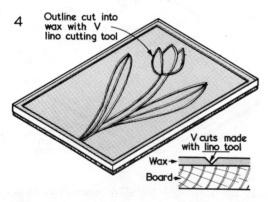

4

Outline cut into wax with V lino cutting tool

V cuts made with lino tool

Wax →
Board →

When the wax has set quite firmly, cut the lines of the design into the wax surface with a V shaped lino cutting tool. The V grooves so formed should be of a regular depth over the whole of the design. Blow or brush off the waste wax as it is cut from the V grooves to avoid trapping the waste where it will interfere with the cutting of the design. The straight lines defining the panel outline should be incised as a V groove in the wax surface, preferably cut against a straight-edge of wood.

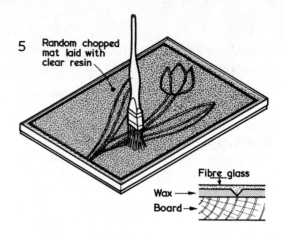

5

Random chopped mat laid with clear resin

Fibre glass

Wax →
Board →

Catalyse sufficient clear resin to form the backing panel. Brush this resin gently into the V grooves and over the surface of the wax. Now lay up a single sheet of random chopped mat glass fibre, stippling the remainder of the prepared clear resin into the mat. Try to avoid air bubbles becoming trapped in the lay-up. When the resin commences to gel, roll a sheet of polyester film over the upper surface of the laid-up fibre glass panel. Place the assembly to one side to set.

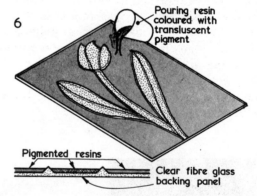

6

Pouring resin coloured with transluscent pigment

Pigmented resins

Clear fibre glass backing panel

Peel off the polyester film and remove the panel backing from the mould. The waste beyond the outline of the panel can be either removed with scissors at the 'green stage' or cut off with hacksaw and filed at a later stage. When the panel backing has set place it level on a table or bench surface. Make up a sufficient number of small quantities of clear resin, each coloured with a few drops of translucent colour pigment. These are each catalysed in turn and carefully poured into the areas surrounded by the V ridges formed on the backing panel. When all the areas have been so coloured, place the panel to one side to set. The resulting translucent panel should be very strong, tough and waterproof.

The photographs on this page show three of the stages in making the fibre glass translucent panel shown on page 67.

Pouring molten wax into the prepared moulding tray. This tray was made from block board 18 mm thick. Masking tape 25 mm wide was fixed around the edges to form a tray about 8 mm deep. An old discarded aluminium saucepan was used as a container in which the paraffin wax could be melted.

Carving the V grooves of the mould with a V lino tool. The straight lines of the outline of the panel have been cut with the lino tool running against the edge of a straight piece of wood. The small brush lying on the pencil drawing was used to brush off waste wax as it was cut from the grooves. Note the practice cuts outside the panel area.

The complete fibre glass backing panel was laid up on the wax mould and has been peeled off after setting for about a day. The waste outside the panel area will be removed with hacksaw and file. The backing will then be ready to receive the translucent pigmented resins to form the colours of the panel.

Table top or wall panels in polyester resins

Decorative layers of coloured polyester resins can be mounted on chipboard or similar panelling material to make up attractive table top or wall panels. Three types of such decorative panels can be made – panels with abstract designs, those showing a marbled effect and those in which a definite pattern or picture effect is required. The chipboard panel provides strength to give toughness and rigidity to the thin and brittle layers of resin. Chipboard is possibly the best material to use for the purpose because the resins will adhere quite firmly to both sides of such board. In addition a further advantage is gained from the stability of chipboard in that it does not shrink or expand readily. Two types of resin are required when undertaking this work – lay-up resin for the decorative skin and panel backing and a clear resin to obtain a smooth surface covering the decorative side. If the edges of the panel are to be covered, a thixotropic resin may also be required. The lay-up resin carries the colour pigments, which are usually opaque. A backing layer of resin is essential to ensure that the chipboard remains flat under the action of the curing of the resins.

When polyester resins polymerize from liquids to fully cured solids shrinking takes place. A skin of resin poured on to a wood-based board and allowed to cure causes the board to become bow shaped in section under the action of the pull of the shrinking resin. To prevent such warping both sides of the boards need to be coated with resin. The shrinkage of each skin counteracts the shrinkage of the other and the board will remain quite flat. Drawing 1 gives a section through a completed decorative panel and shows the various layers of resins required.

Preparation for a panel

The initial stages of preparing any of the three types of panel are shown in Drawing 2. This panel – for the table above – measures 650 mm by 400 mm and was made from 18 mm thick chipboard. About 300 grammes of a blue pigmented lay-up resin were poured into a field formed by applying masking tape around the board edges. This backing was allowed to cure hard. The masking tape was then peeled off, the board turned over and then prepared as in Drawing 2 ready to receive the top decorative layer of resin.

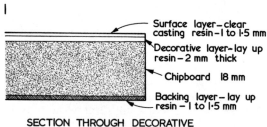

SECTION THROUGH DECORATIVE PANEL

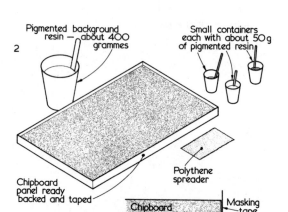

Making the panel

The differences of methods employed for making the decorative resin layers of each of the three types of panel are described below. The preparation of the chipboard is the same with each type and is shown in Drawing 2 on page 70. The finishing top layer is the same in each type of panel. This top layer consists of a clear resin poured over the decorative layer in order to obtain a level, smooth surface finish. This top layer can be made from a pre-activated clear resin as supplied by most manufacturers or can be a clear casting resin as used for making encapsulations.

If clear casting resins are used, it will be remembered that when they cure, the surfaces exposed to the air remain tacky due to the absence of wax in clear casting resins. See page 61. Some suppliers — Trylon Limited for example — will supply a special cobalt based activator which contains some wax. This specially prepared activator, added in small quantities to clear casting resin, will speed up the setting time. It will also allow full polymerization of the surface of the resin — the wax in the activator seals off the air. This ensures that the surface is not tacky when curing is complete. Up to $1\frac{1}{2}\%$ or even 2% of such an activator can be added to clear casting resins for the particular purpose of surfacing table top and wall panels, without undue discolouration taking place.

The decorative resin layer

Abstract design effect

A clear idea of the abstract effect required and the colours to be employed needs to be thought out before the laying of the decorative resins commences. If the usual pre-activated lay-up type of resin is employed, the various colours will tend to merge and disperse into one another as the resins set over the usual 30 to 40 minutes setting time. To fix the design quickly and to prevent this merging and blurring of edges of adjacent colour bands, the setting time can be speeded up by adding a further quantity of activator — up to 2% or even 3% of activator according to the speed of setting desired. This will lessen the setting time to as little as 8 to 10 minutes. The correct — normally cobalt based — type of activator must be added. If an amine activator is mixed in a resin already pre-activated by a cobalt type activator, setting times will be impossibly fast, rapid discolouration of the surface will take place, splits will occur and there will be a danger of fire.

The order of working is:

1   Mix a quantity of lay-up resin with pigment to form the background colour. About 1·25 kilogrammes of resin to the square metre of board is needed. To this add about 60 grammes of pigment to each kilogramme of resin.
2   Mix smaller quantities of resin with pigments for the various colours of the design.
3   Check that the board is level with a spirit level. Adjust if necessary.
4   Add up to 2% or even 3% of activator to each batch of resin and stir in thoroughly.
5   Add 2% of catalyst to the background resin and pour it evenly over the surface of the board — a polythene spreader such as is used to spread glue is a good tool to spread the resin to an even thickness.
6   Add catalyst to the small quantities of colours and pour these in the areas where they are required. Wooden sticks or plastic straws can be used to place and spread the colours and blowing through the straw can assist in forming very pleasing colour effects. Drops of coloured resin can be placed in position with the aid of the straws. The laying of the design must be carried out with some speed because of the quick setting time.
7   Place to one side for the resin to set.

Marbled effect

1   Mix a sufficient quantity of resin for the background colour with the required colour pigment. The same quantities will be needed as for an abstract design background.
2   Mix separate small quantities of resin

with pigments to give the streaky marbling effects.

3 Check that the board is flat with a spirit level and adjust if necessary.

4 Add extra activator to all the resins – up to 2% or even 3% – and mix in thoroughly.

5 Add 2% of catalyst to each of the resin mixes.

6 Pour the small samples of resin into the larger quantity of background resin and swirl the mixture around with a sweep or two of a stirring stick. On no account should the colours be mixed together. The resulting mix should show pronounced stripes and streaks of the smaller quantities of coloured resins quite distinct against the background colour.

7 Pour the mixture as evenly as possible over the whole surface of the board. An even layer can then be formed by allowing the resin to flow by tilting the board in several directions. The board must be set back level after tilting. The resin will settle to a level spread during the 8 to 10 minutes of setting time. The resulting effect should be similar to the streaks and swirls of colour seen in a polished marble.

8 Place to one side for the resin to set.

Picture or design effect

1 Mix sufficient resin with pigment to form a background.

2 Catalyse the resin and spread over the board. There is no need to add extra activator.

3 When the background resin has set – 30 to 40 minutes – the desired picture or design can be painted on to the surface using a pigmented clear resin. Painting brushes of the normal type can be used. Prepare several small containers each containing 20 or 30 grammes of resin. Catalyse each batch of resin with half the usual amount of catalyst – 1% instead of 2%. Spread small quantities of pigments on to a painter's palette board. The brushes are dipped into the catalysed resins and then pigments can be mixed into the resin with the brush on the palette board – in a similar way in which poster paints and water are used for paint-

ing. The resulting resin and colour mix is then painted on to the background resin to form the desired effect. The brushes will need to be cleaned with cleaning fluid when the design has been completed.

4 Place the panel to one side for the resins to set on to a flat surface. Setting will not commence for an hour or longer because of the small quantity of catalyst added to the resins.

Top finishing layer

All three types of panel should be finished in the same manner. When the design layer of resin has set hard, level up the board and spread clear resin over the surface to form a smooth level finish. This surface layer must be allowed to fully cure – four days or longer – before attempting the final polishing process.

Surface finish

When cure is complete, remove the masking tape from the board edges and work the surface flat and smooth with fine wet-and-dry sandpaper. Sprinkle water over the surface to assist the cut of the sandpaper. When a satisfactory flat, smooth surface has been obtained, it can be polished with polyester polishing cream to a glass-like lustre. The polish is applied with waste rag and then burnished with clean dusters until all sandpapering scratches are removed. A lambswool mop in a powered hand drill can be used to burnish the surface. The resulting surface is heat resistant, hard, tough, waterproof and easily cleaned.

Methods of mounting the panels

The panels can either be mounted in frames or on legs for use as tables, or can be fixed to a wall as decorative wall-panels. Some suggested methods of mounting are:

1 As shown in the photograph on page 70. A table frame is made specially for the panel and it is fitted permanently into the frame.

2 A frame can be made from angle iron into which the top is slotted.

3   Mounted on do-it-yourself legs screwed to the underside of the panel. If mounted in this manner, the edges of the panel will need to be finished. Several methods can be adopted:

(*a*) Painting thixotropic resin, pigmented to match the background colour, along the edges.

(*b*) Applying thin strips of hardwood around the edges. These 'lippings' can be glued, or glued and screwed, in position and then polished.

(*c*) Applying edging made of plastic or aluminium as supplied by do-it-yourself shops.

4   If required as a wall panel, the chipboard used need only be 12 mm thick. Such panels can be mounted in a wooden frame or the edges finished with thixotropic resin. The panels can either be hung on chains or cords or screwed permanently to the wall using screws set in Rawlplugs.

The photographs show stages in the making of decorative panels for table tops.

Spreading a backing layer with a polythene spreader.

The background resin for an abstract has been poured. Resin for one of the colours in the design has been added and a third coloured resin is about to be spotted in with a stirring stick.

The decorative layer for a marbled effect has just been laid.

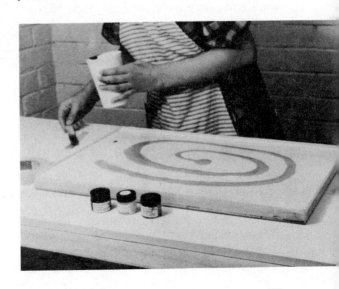

Sculptures in polyester resin

Abstract sculptures or sculptures based on natural forms can be made from polyester resins built up on supporting frames made from suitable materials.

Frame materials

The supporting frames may be made from a variety of materials – wire, wire netting, paper, twine, rags, rope, wood, pieces of metal such as tinplate, polystyrene foam, rigid polyurethane foam. Such materials must be dry and free from grease or oil. Any method of joining the parts of the frames together can be employed – gluing, joining with resin, stapling, nailing, pinning, Sellotaping. The jointing methods need not be particularly strong – the frame will be enclosed in resin reinforced with glass fibre.

Polystyrene foam is attacked and dissolved by polyester resin and is also difficult to shape because it crumbles. It can, however, be used as a frame material if given several coats of emulsion paint.

Two materials of particular value are rigid polyurethane foam and 'paper rope'. Rigid polyurethane foam must not be confused with flexible polyurethane foam as used in upholstery, which is valueless for sculpture frames.

Rigid polyurethane foam is easily worked to shape with sharp knives, files, Surform tools and glasspaper. The dust given off from such working can irritate the skin and eyes. If large amounts of this dust are generated for any length of time it is advisable to wear a mask and goggles.

'Paper rope' is paper wound round a core of wire. The 'rope' can be bent to any required shape which is then retained because of the wire. Both rigid polyurethane foam and paper rope can be obtained from resin suppliers.

Resins, pigments and fillers

Three types of resin are required – gel-coat, thixotropic and lay-up. Fillers to thicken and give body to the resins may be necessary. The cleanest and easiest filler for this purpose is powdered calcium carbonate (chalk), but sand or sawdust can also be used providing they are quite dry. Metallic powders of aluminium, brass or iron or flaked bronze are excellent pigmenting materials for the final surface colour and texture. These metallic pigments should be mixed in about equal volumes of resin and metal. If too little metal powder is in the mix, the resulting finish can be disappointing. Colour pigments can also be used for the final coat of resin.

Making a sculpture

Typical methods of procedure can be shown by describing the making of the bird sculpture shown on page 76.

Preparation

Before commencing work make a pencil drawing of the proposed sculpture. No matter how roughly drawn this sketch is, it will give a clear idea of the proposed final result and assist in estimating shapes and sizes, not only of the whole piece, but also of its parts in relation to each other.

The whole job can be completed in two or three hours, making it advisable to gather together all the materials and tools necessary for the project before starting. A list for the bird sculpture would be:
Polythene sheet to cover work top.
25 mm thick sheet of polyurethane foam.
Some paper rope.
A few 50 mm nails.
Brass strip for the beak.
A piece of wood for the crest.
Gel-coat resin, thixotropic resin and lay-up resin.
Catalyst for the resins.
Some fillers – calcium carbonate.
Some chopped strand glass fibre mat – waste pieces would be quite suitable.
Pigment – in this case flaked bronze.
A 25 mm brush and stirring sticks.
Three mixing bowls.
Barrier cream and disposable polythene gloves.
Knife, rasp (or Surform tool), glasspaper.
A pair of pliers.

The polythene sheet is spread out to protect the work top. Waste resin will set hard on the polythene sheet, from which it can later be peeled to allow the sheet to be re-used.

Cleanliness is essential. Tools, brushes, hands and bench should be kept clean throughout the work. To this end waste rag and cleansing fluid should be near to hand ready to wipe off resin which has adhered to some spot where it is not wanted.

The supporting frame

The base is cut from the rigid polyurethane sheet with a knife and finished to its final shape with a Surform tool and glasspaper. Two holes for the legs are cut into the top of the base with a knife. Cut two lengths of paper rope with pliers and bend to shape for the legs. Cut out pieces of polyurethane foam for the body with a knife and join them together using catalysed resin as an adhesive. Push nails into the joined pieces to hold them together while the resin sets. The nails can be pushed in by hand, no hammering being necessary. Holes for the legs can be cut into the underside of the body with a knife.

Shape the body, neck and head with a Surform tool and glasspaper. Push in the brass strip forming the beak. Push this strip right along the neck to strengthen this fragile part. No drilling is necessary; the metal will push in under hand pressure alone. Now assemble the base, legs, body and head crest using catalysed thixotropic resin as an adhesive. Place the assembly to one side to allow the resin to set.

Gel coat

Apply a brush coat of catalysed gel coat resin over all surfaces of the assembled supporting frame. Allow this coat to set.

Shaping

Mix thixotropic resin with strips of chopped strand mat glass fibre to form a stiff putty-like dough. Add some powdered chalk to stiffen the mix if necessary. A fair quantity of glass fibre is needed to completely reinforce the surfaces of the supporting frame. The dough is catalysed and worked on to the frame with a wooden stirring stick or a palette knife to form the shape of the sculpture. The dough can be pigmented if thought necessary.

Final coat

When the shaped thixotropic and glass fibre dough has set, mix some lay-up resin with an equal volume of flaked bronze, catalyse and apply as a brush coat to the surface of the sculpture. Set aside for the resins to cure.

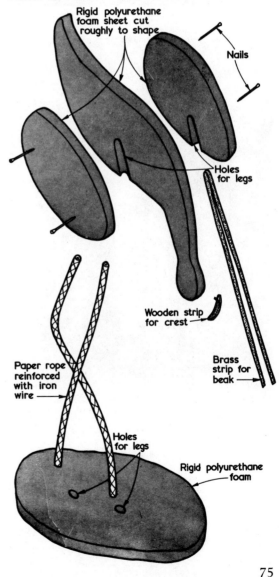

Rigid polyurethane foam sheet cut roughly to shape

Nails

Holes for legs

Wooden strip for crest

Paper rope reinforced with iron wire

Brass strip for beak

Holes for legs

Rigid polyurethane foam

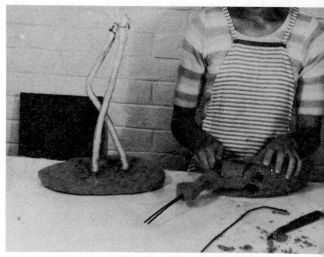

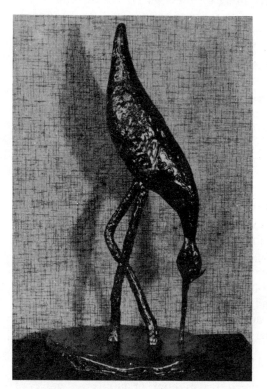

10 Moulding Rubbers

Introduction

Several types of moulding rubber are sold for making moulds in which polyester resins can be cast and from which GRP mouldings may be made. Three of these rubbers are described – 'Vinamold', 'Silastic' free-flowing silicone rubber and 'Silastic' thixotropic silicone rubber. The 'Silastic' series are cured by the addition of catalysts. The 'Silastic' rubbers are not re-usable. 'Vinamold' is suitable for general use and is comparatively cheap. While the 'Silastic' rubbers are expensive they have the advantage that moulds made from them may be used many times without deterioration if care is taken.

No release agents are required when making polyester resin mouldings from these rubber moulds. They are all self-releasing. The models around which the rubber moulds are cast may be made from clay, 'Plasticine', plaster, wood, metal, china, glazed earthenware or any other material at hand. The models may be purpose made or may be existing articles which are to be copied.

The general procedure when making rubber moulds is to secure the model to a base board, build a moulding box around the model from wood, card, metal foil or plaster, cover the model with the rubber to fill the mould box and then place the mould to one side to allow the rubber to set. Other, more advanced methods beyond the scope of this book can be employed. In fact these moulding rubbers are very versatile materials. An exact duplicate of the model's surface is imprinted on the inside of the rubber mould. Because of this, the surfaces of models need to be finished with some care. Unwanted defects are moulded equally as accurately as the desired surface finish.

Vinamold

'Vinamold' is a vinyl based rubber which can be melted and poured to form a mould. After use, the mould can be cut into pieces, remelted and the rubber poured again to form another mould. Remelting can take place about ten times before the rubber deteriorates. It is because 'Vinamold' can be remelted several times that it is cheap moulding material. Its initial cost is also not particularly high. Several grades are sold according to the melting point and hardness of the rubber. The standard grade melts at about 150°C and is made in four hardnesses from very hard (chocolate colour) to soft (blue colour). For use with polyester resins it is advisable to use the 'Special' grade melting at 170°C (natural rubber colour).

Models

Models made from non-porous materials such as clay or 'Plasticine' require no special surface treatment before 'Vinamold' is poured over them. Porous materials such as wood need to be sealed with French polish or clear varnish and then painted with at least two coats of aluminium paint to prevent absorption of the molten rubber into the surface of the model.

Melting

'Vinamold' should be melted slowly – allow about 30 minutes for each ½ kilogramme. Cut the rubber into small pieces and add slowly to the melting pot until all the rubber has been melted. Check temperature with a thermometer if possible. Any metal container is suitable as a melting pot except those made from zinc or copper. The melting pot can be placed inside an air jacket made from any suitably sized tin container to avoid burning the rubber. Whether an air jacket is used or not, the melting rubber needs to be stirred occasionally to prevent burning. Burning shows as a pronounced darkening of the rubber with copious fumes being produced. The melting pot should be covered with a lid to prevent cooling and also to reduce the odours given off. The area in which melting is carried out should be well ventilated.

Pouring

The molten rubber should be poured quickly and evenly into the mould without any pause. Do not pour directly on to the model but to one side so that the rubber flows evenly around the model without air bubbles forming on its surface. When the mould has been poured, place it to one side to allow the rubber to cool and set. Nothing is gained by attempting rapid cooling in a cold water bath.

Silicone rubbers

These rubbers are sold as liquids or pastes which set after a catalyst has been added. Despite their initial high cost they can be of value in craft work when a mould is required from which numerous, accurate mouldings need to be made. The rubbers are not re-usable and when a mould is no longer required it is thrown away. The thin, white 'Silastic' 3110 is a free-flowing rubber which can be poured into a mould. The thick 'Silastic' 504 is a paste which needs to be brushed on to the model being moulded.

When using silicone rubbers, manufacturer's instructions must be followed. Once the catalyst has been added the rubbers will inevitably set. Freshly made moulds need to stand for three days before use.

The head shown in the photograph was made in fibre glass laid inside a mould made from moulding rubbers. The photograph was taken in the showrooms of Trylon Limited of Wollaston.

Making a Vinamold mould

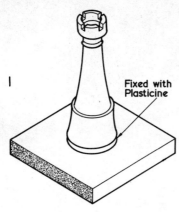

The model, in this case a castle (or rook) from a set of chessmen, is firmly fixed to a base made from wood, card, metal plate or similar material.

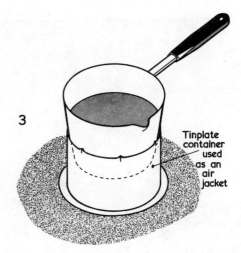

'Vinamold' is cut into small pieces and melted in a suitable container, in this case an old saucepan. To assist in preventing burning the saucepan is placed inside a tin-plate container made from a food 'tin'. Heat is supplied by a gas ring or electrical ring.

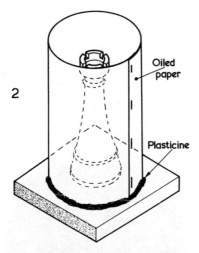

A box, made from wood, metal foil, oiled paper, cardboard or some such material, is formed around the model. The box shown above, made from oiled paper, is stapled together to form a cylinder around the model. The box must be firmly fixed to the base using some material such as 'Plasticine'.

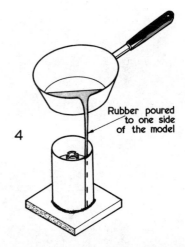

The melted rubber is poured into the mould box. The stream of molten rubber runs into the box to one side of the model to avoid bubbles forming on the surface of the model.

The mould rubber is allowed to cool — overnight. It is then taken off from the base board, turned upside down when it can then be used for casting castle pieces in polyester resin.

A glazed earthenware head placed inside a moulding box. The head is fixed with 'Plasticine' to the base of the box and all corners of the box are sealed, also with 'Plasticine'.

Applying a gel coat inside the completed mould. Flaked bronze has been mixed with the gel coat polyester resin to form a copy of the head with a simulated bronze finish. The base of the mould box has been removed and refixed to the other side of the box.

Pouring the molten 'Vinamold'. The box and glazed head have been warmed slightly over a gas ring to stop the box and head suddenly chilling the hot rubber.

The complete 'bronze' fibre glass moulding released from the mould. Two laminations of glass fibre were laid behind the gel coat once it had gelled.

A 'Plasticine' head, modelled on a piece of 'Contiplas' has been boxed with strips of wood nailed together.

The completed GRP moulded head. In this case aluminium powder was mixed with the gel coat and two laminations of fibre glass laid behind the gel coat. After being released from the mould the surface of the face was polished with metal polish. The mask was glued to a piece of grainy pine with polyester resin.

Pouring the 'Vinamold' around the 'Plasticine' head.

P.–C. & D.—F

Silicone rubber skin mould

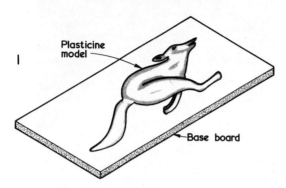

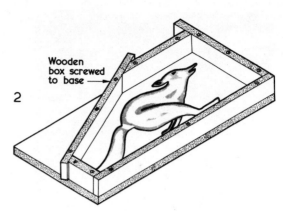

A model of the required shape is made from clay or 'Plasticine'. In this case the relief shape of the running fox was made in 'Plasticine' worked to shape on a piece of wood. 'Contiplas' board – coated with melamine formaldehyde – provides an excellent smooth working surface, but any flat material can be used. Tools made from pieces of wood dowel were used to model the 'Plasticine'. The relief stands about 18 mm high.

Strips of wood are screwed down on to the base board around the relief model to leave a gap of 15 to 20 mm all around. The corners where these strips meet the base board may need sealing with 'Plasticine' to prevent rubber creeping under the strips. 'Contiplas' can again be used to make this box, but any wood or other material – such as cardboard – is suitable.

A GRP moulding made in a silicone rubber skin mould. Powdered brass was mixed with the gel coat and the completed moulding was polished with metal polish before being glued with polyester resin to a teak backboard.

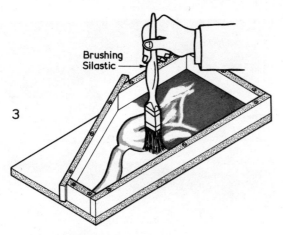

3

A thin brush coat of 'Silastic' red thixotropic silicone rubber mixed with 10% of No. 1 catalyst is stippled over the relief model and into the box corners. Allow this to gel — about eight hours. Brush a second coat of catalysed rubber over the gelled surface, place butter muslin, mutton cloth or similar open-weave fabric over the wet rubber and stipple in more rubber. Repeat until two reinforcing layers of open-weave fabric have been applied.

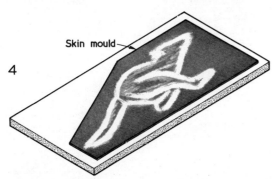

4

When the rubber has set firmly — allow several days — unscrew the box surround. Trim off excess rubber with scissors. This leaves a reinforced rubber skin mould about 3 mm to 4 mm thick overlaying the relief shape on its base board.

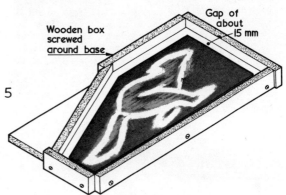

5

Replace the strips of wood as shown leaving a gap all around the skin mould. It may be necessary to use additional strips of wood for this purpose. This forms a box about 20 mm deep with the skin mould at the bottom. This box is now ready to receive a strengthening base for the skin mould made from plaster of Paris and strips of open-weave fabric.

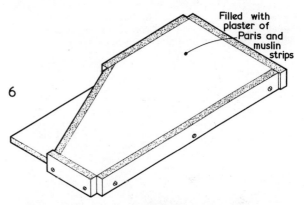

6

Mix plaster of Paris with water and fill the box with the mixture adding strips of open-weave fabric as the box is filled. The strips need to be about 150 mm long by 50 mm wide and are added at random angles within the plaster of Paris. The strips of cloth reinforce the rather brittle plaster and so strengthen it against accidental damage.

Making up the skin mould. Note the vertical stippling brush action which ensures penetration of the rubber through the cloth reinforcement. Note also the disposable polythene gloves.

Laying a gel coat of polyester resin in the skin-mould. In this case the GRP moulding is coloured with a tangerine pigment. Note the polythene sheet on the table.

The skin mould ready for use. The mould box has been unscrewed. The skin mould is quite flexible and the plaster base gives it rigidity.

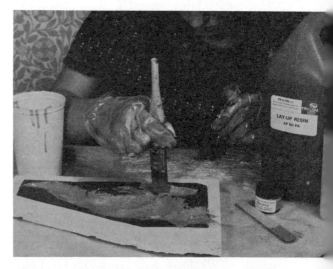

Laying the fibre glass. The glass fibre is cut up into small pieces which are laid with lay-up resin overlapping each other. At the 'green stage' the excess fibre glass is trimmed off with a sharp knife.

Casting in polyester resins

Small articles such as chessmen may be cast by pouring polyester resins into moulds made from a variety of rubber materials. One such moulding rubber is 'Vinamold'. See pages 77 to 81. Other rubbers may be used, two of which are from the 'Silastic' range of vulcanizing silicone rubbers. Both of these 'Silastic' rubbers are expensive to purchase, but produce moulds in which a very large number of identical articles may be cast. 'Vinamold' is only suitable for making moulds when a small number of identical castings are required. 'Silastic' rubbers are not re-usable. One of these two 'Silastic' rubbers was used for making the moulds described here. The second, which is also a free flowing rubber, is not described but is suitable for castings which contain a high degree of undercut, the rubber being very tough and extremely resistant to tear.

Various resins are suitable for making castings. Lay-up resin is fairly satisfactory for small castings when opaque pigments are used to colour the resin. For larger castings, or when translucent pigments are used, clear resins or clear casting resins are to be preferred. Polyester resins shrink as curing proceeds. Splits and cracks may occur as a result, unless some precautions are observed. The rate of cure can be slowed by adding less than the usual 2% of catalyst – even as little as 0·5%. Internal stresses within the curing resins will largely be relieved during this slow rate of cure. Owing to the absence of wax in the formulation of clear casting resins surfaces open to the air are tacky even after curing is complete when these resins are cast. This tackiness can be avoided by rolling polyester film on to surfaces which are open to the air at gel stage. Failing this, sandpapering will cut through the tacky layer to expose the fully cured resin beneath the surface.

Casting a set of chessmen

The series of photographs shows a method of making a mould in 'Silastic' white, free flowing, silicone rubber. The liquid rubber is catalysed with 10% of the appropriate catalyst – supplied in a tube. When freshly catalysed, the mixture can be easily and quickly poured into a moulding box. At least three days must elapse before the mould is used, although the rubber commences setting in three or four hours. This particular moulding rubber may be used to cast pieces with slight undercuts but will tear if deeply undercut castings are attempted.

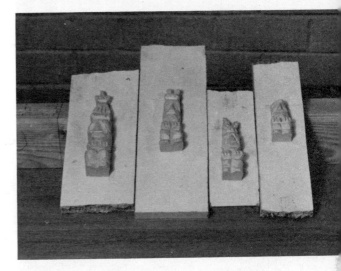

The chessmen were formed in 'Plasticine' on pieces of melamine faced chipboard. The 'Plasticine' can be worked to shape with small knives or with shaped pieces of dowel. This particular group of pieces were an attempt by a secondary school pupil to produce a set of chessmen based on Aztec statuary.

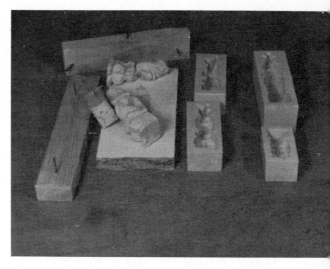

The 'Plasticine' models have each been encased in a wooden casting box. Due regard should be given to economy by making each box as small as practicable. The liquid rubber is being mixed with 10% of catalyst. Thorough mixing is necessary.

The moulding boxes have been taken from the moulds and the 'Plasticine' models removed. The models may become damaged when they are extracted from the moulds, but this is of no concern because exact replicas of their shapes have been produced in the moulds. Although the models can be removed from the moulds when the rubber has set hard, resin must not be poured into the moulds until at least three days have elapsed from the time of pouring the rubber.

Pouring the catalysed rubber into the moulding boxes. The stream of rubber should be directed to one side of the models within the boxes. If poured directly on to the models any slightly undercut portions may be missed because of air bubbles forming which are not driven out by the rubber.

Removing cured chessmen from the moulds. These four pieces were cast in a clear resin tinted with translucent colours. The backs of each piece will be sandpapered smooth and then polished with polyester polish.

11 Plastics used in conjunction with Woodwork

Decorative plastic laminates

Plastic laminate sheets such as 'Formica' are made from the two thermosetting plastics, phenol formaldehyde and melamine formaldehyde, reinforced with paper. These sheets are wear resistant, heat resistant, water resistant and tough. They are suitable for surfacing plywoods, blockboards and chipboards when making items such as table mats, cheese or meat boards, tea trays and kitchen furniture or bathroom furniture.

Manufacture

Drawings 1 to 3 are diagrams showing how plastic laminates are manufactured. Several layers of tough Kraft paper impregnated with phenol formaldehyde provide strength. A good quality paper printed with the design provides the decoration. This and a surfacing layer of cellulose paper are impregnated with melamine formaldehyde. The partly cured, impregnated papers (Drawing 1) are stacked as in Drawing 2. Bonding and curing are then obtained in a press – Drawing 3 – which compresses the layers to a thin sheet.

Cutting and gluing

Plastic laminates can be cut by scoring lines in the upper surface. The sheet is then broken cleanly along the scored line. Special tools can be purchased for this purpose, but any sharp, hard, steel tool will make the scored lines. Hacksaws or fine toothed wood-worker's saws are suitable for cuts other than those made right across or along a sheet.

Rubber based impact glues can be employed to glue plastic laminates. Two methods are shown. Drawings 4a and 4b illustrate one method and the photographs on page 88 show the second.

Apply a thin film of impact glue to both surfaces to be joined. Allow to dry (about 20 minutes). Place the board against two nails projecting from a strip of wood cramped to the bench top. Position the plastic sheet into the corner formed by the board and the wood strip. Lower the sheet to the board. Apply hand pressure firmly all over the surface to ensure good contact and adhesion.

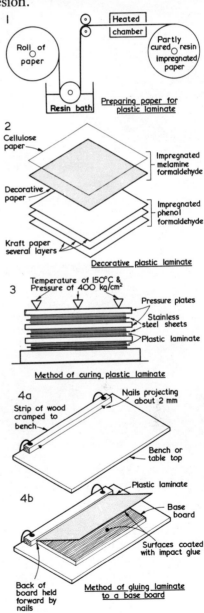

1 Preparing paper for plastic laminate

Roll of paper — Resin bath — Heated chamber — Partly cured resin Impregnated paper

2 Decorative plastic laminate

Cellulose paper — Im: Impregnated melamine formaldehyde — Decorative paper — Impregnated phenol formaldehyde — Kraft paper several layers

3 Method of curing plastic laminate

Temperature of 150°C & Pressure of 400 kg/cm² — Pressure plates — Stainless steel sheets — Plastic laminate

4a Strip of wood cramped to bench — Nails projecting about 2 mm — Bench or table top

4b Plastic laminate — Base board — Surfaces coated with impact glue — Back of board held forward by nails — Method of gluing laminate to a base board

The photographs below show methods of cutting plastic laminate and of gluing the cut sheet to the front surface of a small door. In this case the plastic sheet is a lime green coloured piece of 'Formica'.

Note Two surfaces coated with an impact glue and then allowed to dry will adhere quite firmly to each other when they come into contact. This means that special methods must be employed when gluing with an impact glue.

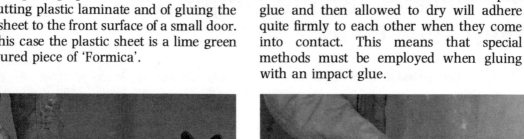

A straight edge – in this case the edge of the door frame – is cramped on to the sheet along the line to be cut. A wood chisel pulled towards the body scores a shallow groove – four or five passes of the chisel.

Impact glue is spread with a thin piece of waste wood. The underside of the plastic sheet will also need to be spread with glue.

By lifting the edge of the sheet upwards, enough pressure is exerted to break the sheet along the scored line. The break could have been made by pressing the sheet across the edge of the bench.

Allow the glue to dry (20 to 30 minutes). Place a piece of paper over the board, and the 'Formica' downwards on to the paper. Now draw the paper out from between the two surfaces. The plastic will adhere to the board as the paper is withdrawn.

Polyurethane foams

Flexible polyurethane foams are materials which can be employed for padding the seats of chairs or stools, for general upholstery work and for making cushions and pillows. This type of cushioning foam is available in a range of densities and hardnesses. The choice of the most suitable density and hardness for any particular piece of work is one which needs to be made with some care if the maximum comfort and long life are to be obtained from the foam. Five typical types, taken from a list of sixteen grades as made by Dunlop Limited, are given below together with the grading colour of each type. Generally, high density foam is suitable for seats and the lower density foams for backs. Chipfoam, made by bonding together small pieces of foam, is of a higher density than those shown in the list below.

Polyurethane foam of this type is polyether foam. Another type of urethane foam, known as polyester foam, is used as thin backings for padded upholstery fabrics. The heavier, close celled polyurethane foam employed to give buoyancy to canoes, to reinforce polyester resins and for flower presentation, is not suitable for upholstery.

Methods of shaping polyether foam for padding simple chair or stool seats are shown, together with a method of making a square edged loose cushion seat to be covered with a pvc coated fabric.

Colour of foam	Density	Hardness	Typical applications
Light green	low	medium	Backs and quiltings
White	low	soft	Pillows
Pale yellow	medium	medium	General purpose upholstery
Gold	high	medium	Seats
Peach	high	hard	Seats in cars and coaches

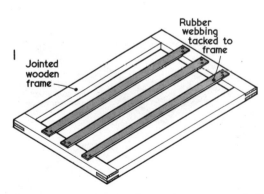

To make a loose seat for a chair or stool. If the polyether foam is less than about 50 mm thick it is advisable to make a wooden frame across which rubber/rayon webbing is stretched and tacked. The extra springiness obtained from the webbing increases the comfort of the foam padding.

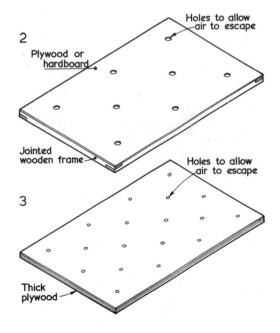

If the foam is more than about 50 mm thick it can be mounted direct on to unsprung frames.

Drawing 2 shows such a frame made by gluing and nailing thin plywood or hardboard to a jointed wooden surround.

Drawing 3 shows a seat made from a single piece of thick plywood.

In both cases holes are bored through the seat boards to allow air to be expelled as the foam is compressed by being sat upon.

If rounded edges are required, glue a wide band of tape along the edges of the foam as in Drawing 5. A rubber based impact glue is suitable for this. The taped foam is then glued to the seat frame and the overhanging tape pulled down and tacked to the seat edges.

All the edges may be shaped in this way although only two are so shown in Drawing 6. This method is suitable for sprung frames.

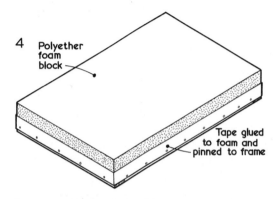

4 Polyether foam block

Tape glued to foam and pinned to frame

If a square edged seat is required glue the foam on to the seat frame with a rubber based impact glue (Bostik or Evostick). A wide tape glued to the edges of the foam and tacked to the seat edges will retain the squareness of the sides.

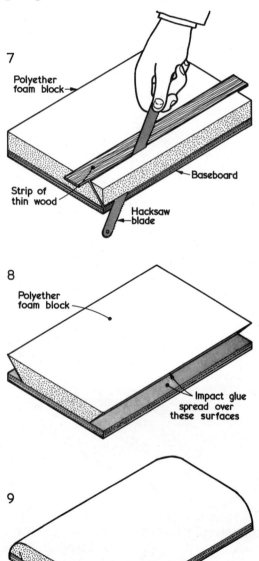

7 Polyether foam block

Strip of thin wood

Hacksaw blade

Baseboard

8 Polyether foam block

Impact glue spread over these surfaces

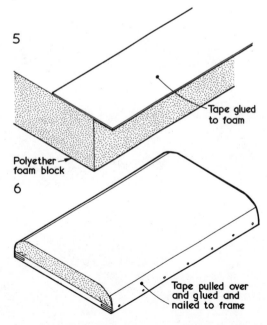

5

Tape glued to foam

Polyether foam block

6

Tape pulled over and glued and nailed to frame

9

Glued surfaces pressed together

Another method of producing rounded seats is shown in the Drawings 7 to 9. First the edges are trimmed to an angle of about 45° as shown in Drawing 7. A straight piece of wood is placed on the foam to guide a hacksaw blade which cuts the 45° chamfer. A sharp knife or a bread saw knife can be used if a hacksaw blade is not available.

The chamfered foam is glued with impact glue to the seat. Impact glue is spread over the chamfers and on the area of the seat beneath the chamfers. When the glue is tacky the chamfered edges are pressed by hand on to the seat board to form the required shape.

A rounded pillow or cushion can be made following the procedure shown in Drawings 10 to 12. Spread impact glue along the edges of the foam. Allow this to become tacky. Then gradually close the cushion edges – Drawing 11 – to produce the rounded edges shown in Drawing 12.

All four edges of the foam can be shaped to form a pillow or cushion rounded on all four edges.

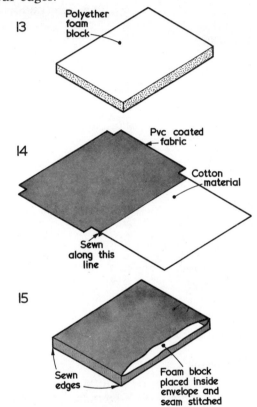

13

Polyether foam block

14

Pvc coated fabric

Cotton material

Sewn along this line

15

Sewn edges

Foam block placed inside envelope and seam stitched

10

Polyether foam block

Impact glue spread over long edges

11

Glued edges pressed together

12

Edges completely glued

To make a loose square edged covered cushion first cut the polyether foam to the required rectangle. Allow an extra 12 mm for every metre length to both length and width of the rectangle.

Now cut pvc coated fabric to shape – Drawing 14 – and sew to it a bottom piece made from cotton material. Sew this combination of pvc fabric and cotton to form an open envelope into which the foam is stuffed. Sew the open end together by hand to complete the seat.

The cotton material allows for the escape of air from the foam when the seat is sat upon.

Appendix

Conversion tables

Abbreviations – S.I.

S.I.	Système International
gramme	g
kilogramme	kg
metre	m
centimetre	cm
millimetre	mm
square centimetre	cm^2
square metre	m^2
cubic centimetre	cm^3
millilitre	ml

Abbreviations – Imperial

ounce	oz.
pound	lb.
inch	in.
foot (feet)	ft.
square inch	in.^{2}
square foot	ft.^{2}

Note Rough conversions usually quite satisfactory for hand craft work are:

28 grammes	=	1 ounce
100 grammes	=	3½ ounces
1 kilogramme	=	2·2 pounds
25 millimetres	=	1 inch
6·5 cm^2	=	1 in.^{2}
1 m^2	=	10·7 ft.^{2}

S.I.	Imperial
28·35 g	1 oz.
453·6 g	1 lb.
1 kg	2·205 lb.
25·4 mm	1 in.
304·8 mm	1 ft.
6·45 cm^2	1 in.^{2}
1 m^2	10·76 ft.^{2}

Millimetres	Inches
10	0·39
20	0·79
30	1·18
40	1·58
50	1·97
60	2·36
70	2·76
80	3·15
90	3·54
100	3·94

Millimetres	Inches
3·2	$\frac{1}{8}$
6·4	$\frac{1}{4}$
9·5	$\frac{3}{8}$
12·7	$\frac{1}{2}$
15·9	$\frac{5}{8}$
19·1	$\frac{3}{4}$
22·2	$\frac{7}{8}$
25·4	1

Millimetres	Inches
25·4	1
50·8	2
76·2	3
101·6	4
127·0	5
152·4	6
177·8	7
203·2	8
228·6	9
254·0	10

Kilogrammes	Pounds
0·028 (28 g)	1 oz.
0·057 (57 g)	2 oz.
0·113 (113 g)	4 oz.
0·227 (227 g)	8 oz.
0·454 (454 g)	1 lb.
2·268	5 lb.
4·536	10 lb.

Measuring out catalyst

When working with polyester resins the resins will only set after catalysts (hardeners) are added. One gramme of liquid catalyst is approximately 1 cubic centimetre (1 millilitre) in volume. From this the following table of quantities is obtained when adding percentages of catalyst to resins by weight. It is more convenient to measure the catalyst by volume.

Each millilitre of liquid catalyst contains approximately 36 drops. When adding catalyst to small quantities of resin it may be easier to measure the quantities by drops from a pen-filler or from a medical eye-dropper.

Resin by weight	Catalyst by volume		
	1%	2%	4%
1 kg	10 ml	20 ml	40 ml
0·5 kg	5	10	20
0·25 kg	2·5	5	10
200 g	2	4	8
100 g	1	2	4
50 g	0·5	1	2
10 lb.	45	90	180
5 lb.	22·5	45	90
2 lb.	9	18	36
1 lb.	4·5	9	18
8 oz.	2·5	5	10
4 oz.	1	2	4
2 oz.	0·5	1	2

Names and addresses of suppliers

Plastics materials can be purchased for the making of small articles in a large number of retail shops throughout the country. Many of these shops will sell the materials in kit form. Difficulty may be experienced in buying some of the items described in this book or in obtaining larger quantities of the more commonly used materials. If such difficulty is experienced, supplies can be obtained from the firms shown in the lists below.

Glass fibre, polyester resins and associated materials

Bondaglass-Voss Limited,
158–164 Ravenscroft Road,
Beckenham, Kent.

Counter retail service.
Mail order service.
Schools and private customers.
Books.

Isopon Inter Chemicals,
Duxons Turn,
Maylands Avenue,
Hemel Hempstead,
Herts. HP2 4SB

Mail order service.
Schools and private customers.

Griffin & George Limited,
P.O. Box 13,
Wembley,
Middlesex. HA0 1LD

Suppliers to educational establishments.

Prima Glassfibre Materials Limited,
Platts Eyot,
Lower Sunbury Road,
Hampton-on-Thames,
Middlesex. TW12 2HF

Counter retail service.
Mail order service.
Schools and private customers.
Canoe moulds.

Strand Glass Company Ltd.,
Branches as follows:

990 Stockport Road,   72 London Road,
Manchester 19.   Southampton, Hants.
444 Stratford Road,   524–526 High Street,
Sparkshill,   Ilford,
Birmingham 11.   Essex.

5 Scotland Street,   159 St Michael's Hill,
Central 5,   Bristol.
Glasgow.

Haigh Avenue,
Whitehall Industrial Estate,
South Reddish,
Stockport,
Cheshire.

Counter retail service.
Mail order service.
Schools and private customers.
Canoe moulds.

Alec Tiranti Limited,
72 Charlotte Street,
London W1P 2AJ

Counter retail service.
Mail order service.
Schools and private customers.

Trylon Limited,
Thrift Street,
Wollaston,
Northants, NN9 7QJ

Counter retail service.
Mail order service.
Schools and private customers.
Canoe moulds.

'Vinamold' and 'Silastic' moulding rubbers

Alex Tiranti Limited,
72 Charlotte Street,
London W1P 2AJ

Counter retail service.
Mail order service.
Schools and private customers.
Books.

Isopon Inter Chemicals,
Duxons Turn,
Maylands Avenue,
Hemel Hempstead,
Herts. HP2 4SB

Mail order service.
Schools and private customers.

Trylon Limited,
Thrift Street,
Wollaston,
Northants. NN9 7QJ

Counter retail service.
Mail order service.
Schools and private customers.

Vacuum forming sheets

Griffin & George Limited,
P.O. Box 13,
Wembley,
Middlesex. HA0 1LD

Suppliers to educational establishments.

Trylon Limited, Thrift Street, Wollaston, Northants. NN9 7QJ	Counter retail service. Mail order service. Schools and private customers.

Dip coating powders

Griffin & George Limited, P.O. Box 13, Wembley, Middlesex. HA0 1LD.	Suppliers to educational establishments.
Trylon Limited, Thrift Street, Wollaston, Northants. NN9 7QJ	Counter retail service. Mail order service. Schools and private customers.

Polyester film

This firm will supply polyester film in bulk to schools. It makes a wide range of clear, metallized and coloured polyester films under the trade mark 'Vapcolex'.

George M. Whiley Limited, Victoria Road, Ruislip, Middlesex.	*Retail agent:* Paperchase Limited, 216 Tottenham Court Road, London W.1.

Small machines for plastic forming

Griffin & George Limited, P.O. Box 13, Wembley, Middlesex. HA0 1LD	Suppliers to educational establishments.
The Small Power Machine Company Limited, Bath Road, Industrial Estate, Chippenham, Wiltshire. SN14 0BR	Schools, industry and general public.

General

Crafts Unlimited,
The Old Mill,
Nannerch,
Nr Mold,
Flintshire, N. Wales.
and at:
21 Macklin Street,
London W.C.2.
	Counter retail service.
	Mail order service.
	Schools and private customers.
	Suppliers of polyester resins for embedding,
	    lacquering and dipping.
	
	Suppliers of materials for a wide range of
	    other crafts.

Westby Products,
School Lane,
East Keswick,
Nr Leeds. LS17 9DA

Counter retail service.
Mail order service.
Schools and private customers.
Suppliers of polyester resin, 'Vinamold',
    moulds for plastics and material for
    other crafts.

Acrylic sheet

G. H. Bloore Limited,
480 Honeypot Lane,
Stanmore,
Middlesex. HA7 1JT
and branches at:

Mail order service.
Schools and private customers.

G. H. Bloore Limited,
Unit 25,
Chantry Estate Farm,
Kempston, Beds.

G. H. Bloore Limited,
68 Willow Walk,
Bermondsey,
London S.E.1.

G. H. Bloore Limited,
Cater Road,
Bishopworth,
Bristol 3.

G. H. Bloore Limited,
Lawlay Street,
Birmingham 4.

G. H. Bloore Limited,
Solent Road,
Havant,
Hants.

G. H. Bloore Limited,
14 Midland Street,
Manchester.

Cornelius Chemical Company Limited,
Ibex House,
Minories,
London EC3N 1HY

'Plexiglas' sheet, rods and tubes and
    'Makrolon' polycarbonate sheeting.
Will supply direct to schools.

S. O. Department,
Rohm and Haas (U.K.) Ltd.,
Lennig House,
2 Masons Avenue,
Croydon CR9 3NB

'Oroglas' school packs of sheet acrylic
    supplied direct to schools.
'Oroglas' cutting tools also supplied to
    schools.

'Oroglas' school packs are also available
to schools through:
Griffin and George Limited,
P.O. Box 13,
Wembley,
Middlesex. HA0 1LD